WATCHWORDS

ONE

Michael & Peter Benton

Hodder and Stoughton

London Sydney Auckland Toronto

WATCHWORDS

Roger McGough

watch the words
watch words the
watchword is
watch words are   away.
sly as boots
ifyoutakeyoureyesoffthemforaminute

they're   up   and

                                                allover

                                    the

                                                            place

watch

how

chat

or

a   ?

WATCHWORDS

WEST HOVE MIDDLE SCHOOL

How many words can you make out of our title?

Arrange your words in columns according to how many letters each one has but don't use plurals or the names of people or places. Here are some to start you off.

We have juggled 150 so far.
Is this a record?

Contents

The last twenty-five years are often thought of as a golden age of children's literature, a phrase that indicates the high quality of many of the stories written for children but which, in the minds of many teachers and parents, ignores the increasing amount of good poetry available to a young audience. The nineteen-seventies, in particular, have seen established poets such as Ted Hughes, Roy Fuller, Elizabeth Jennings and Charles Causley publishing slim volumes for children as well as the emergence of younger poets, notably Roger McGough, Michael Rosen and Brian Patten, whose verses have a wry, humorous voice that readily appeals to youngsters. The time seem right to present a selection of poetry for children which draws generously upon the work of these contemporary writers and places their poems alongside the best material from earlier periods.

The poems in **Watchwords** have been chosen with the interests and abilities of children between the ages of eight and thirteen in mind. Volume One focuses on the younger end of this age range, Volume Two provides material for the middle years and Volume Three contains poems of greater subtlety, suitable for children at the upper end of primary or middle school as well as those in the early years of secondary school. The material is arranged thematically with suggestions for various activities at the end of each section. It is important for the teacher to present such activities carefully. As they stand, they are no more than starting-points for talking, writing or drama. It is intended that the teacher should select, adapt and modify these ideas in the light of his or her closer understanding of the needs and abilities of the children. Above all, poetry with children should be fun which is why we have included many poems of a light-hearted and humorous tone and why our suggestions for writing often involve children in playing word-games, riddling, inventing shape-poems and the like. Reading and talking about poems lead naturally into children's own writing. In poetry, more than anywhere else, the first two R's should complement each other.

M.G. BENTON
P. BENTON

Me and the
Things I do

POCKETS

Brian Lee

'Come on, where have you put it?
Turn out your pockets . . .
If you can't find it,
You'll never get home.'

An old grey hanky,
An Irish ha'penny,
A coil of string,
And an old brass ring —
A peppermint chew
(Half for me, half for you),
A piece of wire,
A dinky-car tyre,
My bicycle clips
And two poker-chips,
An old rubber, gone hard,
And a cigarette card
(Extremely rare) —
No, it's not there.

'Well, where *have* you put it? —
Try the left-hand pocket.
No wonder you've lost it.
The bus hasn't gone yet.'

A big paper clip
And a lead battleship,
An elastic band
And a pinch of sand
Still there from last summer,
A pencil sharpener,
Glass marbles, a pin,
A box for keeping things in —
Empty — a whistle
And a tiny pistol
From a Christmas cracker,
A bit of sherbet sucker,
My two old front teeth —
And underneath —

I've got it, I've got it —
My five penny bit.

'The bus still hasn't gone,
Be quick now, and run!

And now that we're on,
Swap you something of yours
For something of mine.'

'No. No one can have them.
They're mine, they're all mine.'

THE BROKEN TOYS

James Kirkup

In the broken box
The broken toys—
  Dusty,
Battered and rusty,
Tattered and torn,
  Forlorn, forlorn.

The snapped strings
And the busted springs,
The rag-doll raggy and rent,
The pink tin teaset buckled and bent,
  The crashed plane,
  The car, the train—
Smashed in a terrible accident.

And all the dolls' eyes
Rolling loose like heavy marbles
Up the doll's house stairs and down
The stairs of the overturned house . . .
The dead wheels of a clockwork mouse . . .

In the broken box
The broken toys—
  Dusty,
Battered and rusty,
Tattered and torn,
  Forlorn, forlorn.

from **THE RIGHT SORT OF BED**

Sylvia Plath

The *right* sort of Bed
(If you *see* what I mean)
Is a Bed that might
Be a Submarine

Nosing through water
Clear and green,
Silver and glittery
As a sardine

Or a Jet-Propelled Bed
For visiting Mars
With mosquito nets
For the shooting stars.

If you get hungry
In the middle of the night
A Snack Bed is good
For the appetite—

With a pillow of bread
To nibble at
And up at the head
An automat

Where you need no shillings,
Just a finger to stick in
The slot, and out come
Cakes and cold chicken.

Another Bed
That fills the bill
Is the sort of Bed
That is Spottable—

With blankets all splotches
Of black, blue and pink
So nobody'll notice
If you spill ink

Or if the dog and the cat
And the parakeet
Dance on the covers
With muddyish feet

In a Spottable Bed
It *never* matters
Where jam rambles
And where paint splatters!

On the other hand,
If you want to *move*
A Tank Bed's the Bed
Most movers approve.

A Tank Bed's got cranks
And wheels and cogs
And levers to pull
If you're stuck in bogs.

A Tank Bed's treads
Go upstairs or down.
Through duck ponds or through
A cobbledy town.

And you're snug inside
If it rains or hails.
A Tank Bed's got
Everything but sails!

I'M ALONE IN THE EVENING

Michael Rosen

I'm alone in the evening
when the family sits
reading and sleeping
and I watch the fire in close
to see flame goblins
wriggling out of their caves
for the evening

Later I'm alone
when the bath has gone cold around me
and I have put my foot
beneath the cold tap
where it can dribble
through valleys between my toes
out across the white plain of my foot
and bibble bibble into the sea.

I'm alone
when mum's switched out the light
my head against the pillow
listening to ca thump ca thump
in the middle of my ears.
It's my heart.

WHO'S THAT?

James Kirkup

Who's that
stopping at
my door in the
dark, deep
in the dead of the moonless night?

Who's
that in the quiet
blackness,
darker than dark?

Who
turns the han-
dle of my door, who
turns the old brass hand-
le of
my door with never a sound, the handle
that always
creaks and rattles and
squeaks but
now
turns
without a sound, slowly
slowly
    slowly
       round?

Who's that moving through the floor
as if it were a lake, an open door? Who
is it who passes through
what can never be passed through,
who passes through
the rocking-chair
without rocking it,
who passes through
the table without knocking it, who
walks out of the cupboard without unlocking it?
Who's that? Who plays with my toys
with no noise, no
noise?

Who's that? Who is it
silent and silver
as things in mirrors, who's
as slow as feathers,
shy as the shivers,
light as a fly?

Who's that who's that
as close as
close as a hug, a kiss—

Who's THIS?

JOAN WHO HATES PARTIES

John Walsh

Today's little Doreen's party-day;
And it all begins when I'm snatched from play
By Mother, who cries with a gay little laugh,
'Now come along first and have a nice bath!'
And off come my jeans and I'm dumped straight in,
And splashed all over from toes to chin;
Then dumped out again on the big bath-mat—
And don't I just hate that!

For the next half-hour I am rubbed rough-dry,
And tickled with talc till I'm ready to cry,
And perched half-dressed on a backless chair
For the fight between Mother and me and my hair;
Then on go the shoes and the clean white socks,
And the dreamiest of dream-like nylon frocks,
With a sweet blue bow for the end of my plait—
And don't I just hate that!

But I'm ready at last; and at ten-past four
I'll be dropped at dear little Doreen's door;
And at Doreen's door I'll be met with a hearty
Welcome to dear little Doreen's party;
But they won't see me — they won't see Joan —
But a girl with a heart like a thunder-stone;
A girl with the face of a fierce tom-cat . . .
And won't they just hate that!

END OF A GIRL'S FIRST TOOTH

Roy Fuller

Once she'd a tooth that wiggled;
Now she's a gap that lisps.
For weeks she could only suck lollies;
Now she champs peanuts and crithsps.

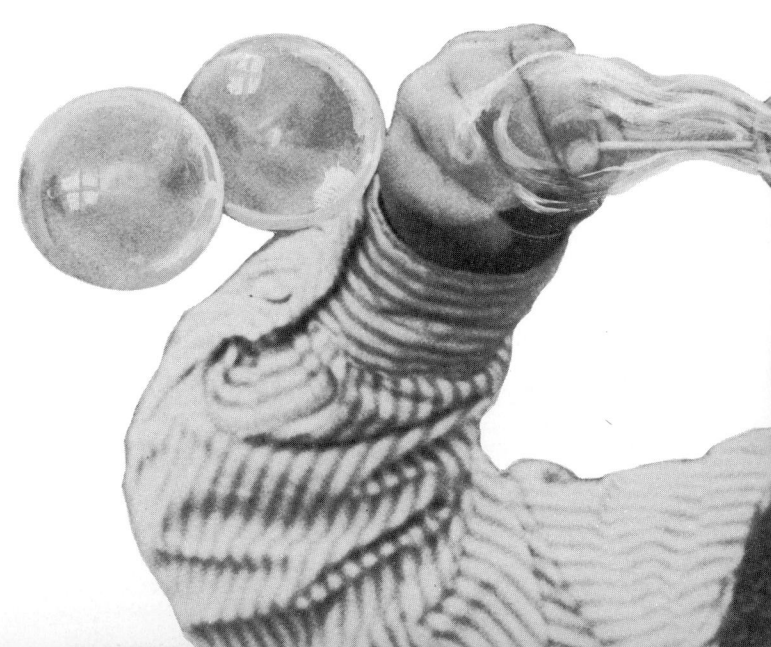

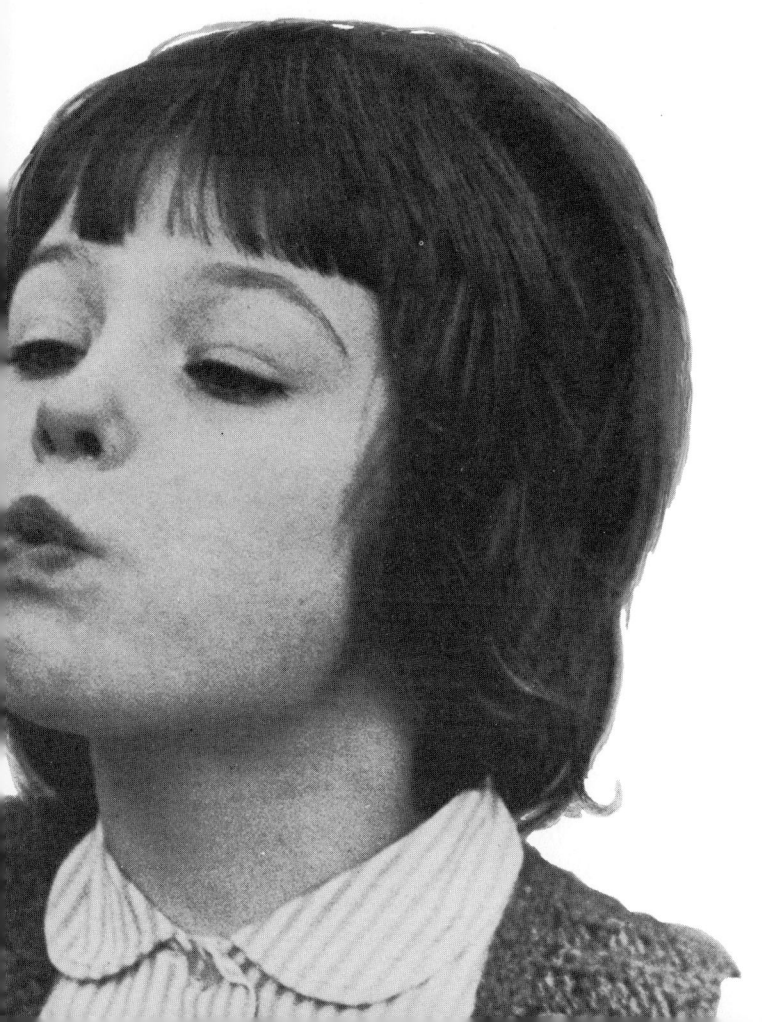

from **A SONG ABOUT MYSELF**

John Keats

There was a naughty Boy
  A naughty Boy was he
He would not stop at home
He could not quiet be—
    He took
    In his Knapsack
    A Book
    Full of vowels
    And a shirt
    With some towels—
    A slight cap
    For night cap—
    A hair brush
    Comb ditto
    New Stockings
    For old ones
    Would split O!
    This Knapsack
    Tight at's back
    He rivetted close
And follow'd his Nose
    To the North
    To the North
And follow'd his nose
    To the North.

There was a naughty Boy
  And a naughty Boy was he
He ran away to Scotland
  The people for to see—
    There he found
    That the ground
    Was as hard
    That a yard
    Was as long,
    That a song
    Was as merry,
    That a cherry
    Was as red—
    That lead
    Was as weighty
    That fourscore
    Was as eighty
    That a door
    Was as wooden
    As in England—
    So he stood in
    His shoes
    And he wonder'd
    He stood in his
    Shoes and he wonder'd.

BUS TO SCHOOL

John Walsh

Rounding the corner
It comes to a stay.
Quick! Grab a rail!
Now we're off on our way . . .
Oh, but it's Thursday,
The day of fear!—
Three hateful lessons!
And school draws near.

Here in the bus though
There's plenty to see:

Boys full of talk about
Last night's TV;
Girls with their violins,
Armfuls of twigs
And flowers for teacher;
Bartlett and Biggs;
Conductor who chats with them,
Jokes about cricket;
Machine that flicks out
A white ribbon of ticket . . .
Yes, but it's Thursday,
The day of fear!—
Six hateful lessons!
And school draws near.

Conductor now waiting,
Firm as a rock,

For Billy, whose penny's
Slid down in his sock.
Conductor frowning,
With finger on handle;
Poor Billy blushes,
Undoes his sandal . . .
'Hold very tight, please!
Any more fares?'
Whistling conductor
Goes clumping upstairs . . .
Boots up above, now!
Boys coming down! . . .
Over the hump-bridge
And into the town.

Old Warren sweeping
In his shirt-sleeves!
Sun on his shop-front,
Sun on the leaves . . .
Only, it's Thursday,
The day of fear!—
All hateful lessons!
And school draws near.

THE MARROG

R. C. Scriven

My desk's at the back of the class
   And nobody, nobody knows
     I'm a Marrog from Mars
With a body of brass
   And seventeen fingers and toes.

Wouldn't they shriek if they knew
   I've three eyes at the back of my head
   And my hair is bright purple
My nose is deep blue
   And my teeth are half-yellow, half-red.

My five arms are silver, and spiked
   With knives on them sharper than spears.
I could go back right now, if I liked —
   And return in a million light-years.

I could gobble them all
For I'm seven foot tall
   And I'm breathing green flames from my ears.

Wouldn't they yell if they knew,
   If they guessed that a Marrog was here?
Ha-ha, they haven't a clue—
   Or wouldn't they tremble with fear!
'Look, look, a Marrog'
   They'd all scream—and SMACK
The blackboard would fall and the ceiling would crack
   And teacher would faint, I suppose.
But I grin to myself, sitting right at the back
   And nobody, nobody knows.

LOST IN A SHOP

John Walsh

From the noisiest end of the crowded store—
Hear that! What a dismal wail!
A little lost girl, stood up on the counter,
As though she were there for sale!

An anxious shop-girl presses her hand;
Her tears fall thickly;
The anxious assistants stare all round . . .
Oh, come someone, and find her quickly!

Talking and Writing

— The poem about pockets on page 8 says that children sometimes carry a very odd mixture of things around with them. Well, do they? Turn out your pockets. Make a list of everything. At the end can you say which is the best thing and why you like it?

— Do any of you have a teddy bear like the one hanging out to dry on page 10? What's your favourite toy? Write a description of it and say what you feel about it. Perhaps you could draw it as well.

— Sylvia Plath, in her poem on page 11, imagines a bed that can do all sorts of things. What is the *right* sort of bed for you?

— Everyone has been frightened at some time by the dark and by strange shapes or sounds that they have imagined. Write down the one that frightens you most, like this:

'The branches outside the window scratch on the glass like someone trying to get in.'

'The coat hanging on the door is like a monstrous black bat.'

Perhaps you could make up a class poem in which everyone adds one idea.

— The little girl in the picture on page 12 has a special place where she likes to go to play on her own. She is using some old clothes in the attic for her dressing-up games. When do you like being on your own? Do you have a special place?

— The children in the poem on page 16 come to school on the bus each day. How do you get to school? Write down what you see and do on the journey. What do you like and dislike about it?

My
Friends

COLD FEET

Brian Lee

They have all gone across
They are all turning to see
They are all shouting 'come on'
They are all waiting for me.

I look through the gaps in the footway
And my heart shrivels with fear,
For far below the river is flowing
So quick and so cold and so clear

And all that there is between it
And me falling down there is this:
A few wooden planks — not very thick —
And between each, a little abyss.

The holes get right under my sandals.
I can see straight through to the rocks.
And if I don't look, I can feel it,
Just there, through my shoes and my socks.

Suppose my feet and my legs withered up
And slipped through the slats like a rug?
Suppose I suddenly went very thin
Like the baby that slid down the plug?

I know that it cannot happen
But suppose that it did, what then?
Would they be able to find me
And take me back home again?

They have all gone across
They are all waiting to see
They are all shouting 'come on' —
But they'll have to carry me.

WORDS

Brian Lee

Sticks and stones
May break my bones
But words can never hurt me —
That is what I'm supposed to say.

But:
'One, two, three,
Bri-an Lee—
His mother picks his fleas,
She roasts them,
She toasts them,
They have them for their teas.'

Sticks and stones
May break my bones
But words can never hurt me—
That is what I say.

But:
'One, two, three,
Bri-an Lee
Went to sea—

A big fish swam up
Got him by the knee.
The boat turned over
Brian couldn't swim
I wonder whatever
Happened to him.'

Sticks and stones
May break my bones
But . . .

'One, two, three,
Bri-an Lee
Went for a pee—
Never came back.
Found him later
Put him in a sack.'

Sticks and stones . . .

But . . .
Words can prick
Can pierce, can sting,
Can cut, can stab
Can scar, can cling:
This is what I shout back —

'Georgie Rudden
Is fat as a pig
He eats so much pudden
His belly gets big.'

'Mary McVickers'
Brain's gone numb
When she bends over
We can all see her bum.
She's forgot to put them on —
No-nickers
Mary McVickers.'

'Freddie Bell
's got feet that smell —
He won't change his socks.
Shut him in a cell,
Drop him down a well,
Nail him in a box.'

But . . .
Nothing I say
Is ever good enough
To hurt them as much
As they hurt me,
Though we stand and shout
Till someone comes out
And tells us to clear off.

Sticks and stones
May break my bones —
With a pound of plaster
Your bones get better —
But once it's been heard,
Who forgets the Word?

I WENT OUT AND LOOKED ABOUT

Michael Rosen

ME: I went out and looked about
        and saw a broken pram.

YOU: I went out and looked about
        and saw the derby ram.

ME: For sale in the market:
        a broken pram on broken wheels,
        hot dogs and jellied eels,
        a blue car with parking lights
        but nowhere free to park it.

YOU: In a field on a farm:
        the derby ram and all his sheep,
        two cows fast asleep
        and swallows swooping in and out
        the shadows in the barn.

BOTH: We went out and looked about.
        We went walking round.

YOU: I went up the country.
ME: I went down the town.

A BOY'S FRIEND

Roy Fuller

I have a secret friend
With whom I never quarrel.
I'm Watson to his Holmes,
He's Hardy to my Laurel.

I'm greedy for his calls
And leave him with sad heart.
He thinks of marvellous games.
He mends what comes apart.

Though when he isn't here
I can't recall his face,
I'm always glancing at
That slightly freckled space.

His name's quite ordinary
But seems unusual.
His brain's stocked like a shop.
His talk is comical.

Often with other friends
Play ends in biffs and screams:
With him, play calmly goes
Through dusk — and even dreams.

FRIENDS

Elizabeth Jennings

I fear it's very wrong of me,
And yet I must admit,
When someone offers friendship
I want the *whole* of it.
I don't want everybody else
To share my friends with me.
At least, I want *one* special one,
Who, indisputably,

Likes me much more than all the rest,
Who's always on my side,
Who never cares what others say,
Who lets me come and hide
Within his shadow, in his house —
It doesn't matter where —
Who lets me simply be myself,
Who's always, *always* there.

THE SECRET BROTHER

Elizabeth Jennings

Jack lived in the green-house
When I was six,
With glass and with tomato plants,
Not with slates and bricks.

I didn't have a brother,
Jack became mine.
Nobody could see him,
He never gave a sign.

Just beyond the rockery,
By the apple-tree,
Jack and his old mother lived,
Only for me.

With a tin telephone
Held beneath the sheet,
I would talk to Jack each night.
We would never meet.

Once my sister caught me,
Said, 'He isn't there.
Down among the flower-pots
Cramm the gardener

Is the only person.'
I said nothing, but
Let her go on talking.
Yet I moved Jack out.

He and his old mother
Did a midnight flit.
No one knew his number:
I had altered it.

Only I could see
The sagging washing-line
And my brother making
Our own secret sign.

HORRIBLE THINGS

Roy Fuller

'What's the horriblest thing you've seen?'
Said Nell to Jean.

'Some grey-coloured, trodden-on plasticine;
On a plate, a left-over cold baked bean;
A cloak-room ticket numbered thirteen;
A slice of meat without any lean;
The smile of a spiteful fairy-tale queen;
A thing in the sea like a brown submarine;
A cheese fur-coated in brilliant green;
A bluebottle perched on a piece of sardine.
What's the horriblest thing *you've* seen?'
Said Jean to Nell.

'Your face, as you tell
Of all the horriblest things you've seen.'

Talking and Writing

— Sometimes you must quarrel with your friends, or want to make friends with someone new, or make up an imaginary friend to play with. Choose the title 'The Quarrel', or 'Making Friends' or 'My Secret Friend' and describe your feelings about one of these.

— In the poem *Cold Feet* on page 20 the boy is frightened to cross the planks over the river. Have you ever been frightened by something like this? Have you ever been 'dared' by your friends to take risks? Think of a time when it happened and write about it.

— Read the poem *Horrible Things* on page 24. What's the most horrible thing you have seen? Perhaps every member of the class could make up one line for a class poem.

— The children in the photographs on pages 20 and 23 have found two very different places in which to play. Where do you play? Talk about your favourite place to play and write down what you like about it.

My
Family

IF YOU DON'T PUT YOUR SHOES ON

Michael Rosen

If you don't put your shoes on before I count fifteen
then we won't go to the woods to climb the chestnut
One
  But I can't find them
Two
  I can't
They're under the sofa three
  No
  O yes
Four five six
  Stop — they've got knots they've got knots
You should untie the laces when you take your shoes
  off seven
  Will you do one shoe while I do the other
  then?
Eight but that would be cheating
  Please
All right
  It always . . .
Nine
  It always sticks — I'll use my teeth
Ten
  It won't it won't
  It has — look.
Eleven
  I'm not wearing any socks

Twelve
  Stop counting stop counting. Mum where
  are my socks mum
They're in your shoes. Where you left them.
  I didn't
Thirteen
  O they're inside out and upside down and
  bundled up
Fourteen
  Have you done the knot on the shoe you
  were . . .
Yes
Put it on the right foot
  But socks don't have right and wrong foot
The shoes silly
Fourteen and a half
  I am I am. Wait.
  Don't go to the woods without me
  Look that's one shoe already
Fourteen and threequarters
  There
You haven't tied the bows yet
  We could do them on the way there
No we won't fourteen and seven eighths
  Help me then
  You know I'm not fast at bows
Fourteen and fifteen sixteenths
  A single bow is all right isn't it
Fifteen we're off
  See I did it.
  Didn't I?

PETER

Eleanor Farjeon

It's all very well, said Peter to Mike,
To say Be brave! but how would you like
When the water runs out with a *glug-glug-glug*,
How would *you* like to be sucked down the Plug?

Next year, when I am as big as you,
I'll sit it out to the finish too,
See if I don't! and let it run
Away till the very last drop is done.

And the squelchy sound it makes in the hole
Won't bother me then, upon my soul!
But this year it's all very well to sneer—
Just you remember yourself last year.

You've *forgot* how the hole gets bigger and bigger
Till it's bigger around than your own figure!
It's so long ago, you've *forgot* what it's like,
That's what it is, said Peter to Mike.

And I *will* get out when the water goes *glug!*
And I *won't* be sucked down the Bathroom Plug!

'FATHER SAYS'

Michael Rosen

Father says
Never
let
me
see
you
doing
that
again
father says
tell you once
tell you a thousand times
come hell or high water
his finger drills my shoulder
never let me see you doing that
again

My brother knows all his phrases off by heart
so we practise them in bed at night

BROTHER AND SISTER

Lewis Carroll

'Sister, sister, go to bed!
Go and rest your weary head.'
Thus the prudent brother said.

'Do you want a battered hide,
Or scratches to your face applied?'
Thus his sister calm replied.

'Sister, do not raise my wrath.
I'd make you into mutton broth
As easily as kill a moth!'

The sister raised her beaming eye
And looked on him indignantly
And sternly answered, 'Only try!'

Off to the cook he quickly ran.
'Dear cook, please lend a frying-pan
To me as quickly as you can.'

'And wherefore should I lend it you?'
'The reason, Cook, is plain to view.
I wish to make an Irish stew.'

'What meat is in that stew to go?'
'My sister'll be the contents!'
        'Oh!'
'You'll lend the pan to me, Cook?'
        'No!'
Moral: Never stew your sister.

MY BACK-SCRATCHER

Brian Lee

I like my back scratched as much as Bones does,
As he wriggles, and writhes, and falls
(He enjoys it so much he can't stand) —
At night before bed when I sit by the fire,
In pyjamas, hot chocolate in my hand.

And Grandma's the one who does it the best —
Mum's nails are too long, her palms are too smooth
And she's much too much to do.
And Dad's a bit rough, and Grandfather's busy,
(He *has* to get down to *The Good Men and True).*

But Grandma's gentle, and she doesn't miss bits,
Her hands are warm, and delightfully rough —
'From scrubbing,' she says, 'and cleaning the grate,
From a lifetime's work for the likes of you:
It's *that*, that makes them first-rate.'

UNCLE FERGIE

Roger McGough

Uncle Fergie
was a famed caber tosser.

As a caber tosser
he had no peer.

It is rumoured
he could toss a caber

from there

to here.

MY AUNT

Ted Hughes

You've heard how a green thumb
Makes flowers come
Quite without toil
Out of any old soil.

Well, my Aunt's thumbs were green.
At a touch, she had blooms
Of prize Chrysanthemums —
The grandest ever seen.

People from miles around
Came to see those flowers
And were truly astounded
By her unusual powers.

One day a little weed
Pushed up to drink and feed
Among the pampered flowers
At her water-can showers.

Day by day it grew
With ragged leaves and bristles
Till it was tall as me or you —
It was a King of Thistles.

'Prizes for flowers are easy,'
My Aunt said in her pride.
'But was there ever such a weed
The whole world wide?'

She watered it, she tended it,
It grew alarmingly.
As if I had offended it,
It bristled over me.

'Oh Aunt!' I cried. 'Beware of that!
I saw it eat a bird.'
She went on polishing its points
As if she hadn't heard.

'Oh Aunt!' I cried. 'It has a flower
Like a lion's beard —'
Too late! It was devouring her
Just as I had feared!

Her feet were waving in the air —
But I shall not proceed.
Here ends the story of my Aunt
And her ungrateful weed.

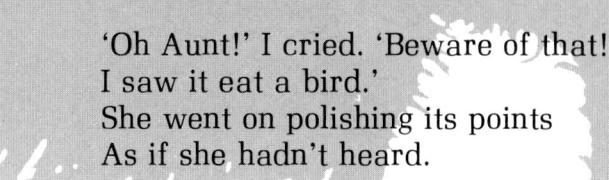

THE NATIONAL UNION OF CHILDREN

Roy Fuller

NUC has just passed a weighty resolution:
'Unless all parents raise our rate of pay
This action will be taken by our members
(The resolution comes in force today):-

'Noses will not be blown (sniffs are in order),
Bedtime will get preposterously late,
Ice-cream and crisps will be consumed for breakfast,
Unwanted cabbage left upon the plate,

'Earholes and finger-nails can't be inspected,
Overtime (known as homework) won't be worked,
Reports from school will all say "Could do better",
Putting bricks back in boxes may be shirked.'

THE NATIONAL ASSOCIATION OF PARENTS

Roy Fuller

Of course, NAP's answer quickly was forthcoming
(It was a matter of emergency),
It issued to the Press the following statement
(Its Secretary appeared upon TV):-

'True that the so-called Saturday allowance
Hasn't kept pace with prices in the shops,
But neither have, alas, parental wages:
NUC's claim would ruin kind, hard-working Pops.

'Therefore, unless that claim is now abandoned,
Strike action for us, too, is what remains;
In planning for the which we are in process
Of issuing, to all our members, canes.'

Talking and Writing

— *'We'll see.'*
'Because I say so.'
'Just wait until your father gets home!'
'Go and ask mummy.'
'Not now, darling . . .'
'Only if you put your coat on!'

Michael Rosen's two poems on pages 28 and 29 are made up from the things that his parents were always saying to him. Make a list of the phrases that your parents are always using.

Compare your list with those of your friends. Can you act out a conversation using as many of these phrases as possible?

— The two poems on pages 29 and 31 are about brothers and sisters. Try to describe your own brother or sister by writing down what they do and what you like and dislike about them. Begin your writing with 'My brother is . . . ' or 'My sister is . . .'.

— Our relatives are often a strange mixture of people. Do you have a favourite relative who you look forward to seeing, or any who make you feel a bit uncomfortable? What does he or she look like and say and do? Describe one of your relatives as vividly as you can.

— What would you like to add to the list of demands made by *The National Union of Children* on page 34? What do you think the parents' replies would be? Could half your group be the children and half be the parents and each side make a speech?

Curiouser
and Curiouser

'AS TO POETRY, YOU KNOW!'

Lewis Carroll

"As to poetry, you know," said Humpty Dumpty, stretching out one of his great hands, "I can repeat poetry as well as other folk, if it comes to that — "

"Oh, it needn't come to that!" Alice hastily said, hoping to keep him from beginning.

"The piece I'm going to repeat," he went on without noticing her remark, "was written entirely for your amusement."

Alice felt that in that case she really *ought* to listen to it; so she sat down, and said "Thank you" rather sadly.

> "In winter, when the fields are white,
> I sing this song for your delight—

only I don't sing it," he added, as an explanation.

"I see you don't," said Alice.

"If you can *see* whether I'm singing or not, you've sharper eyes than most," Humpty Dumpty remarked severely. Alice was silent.

> "In spring, when woods are getting green,
> I'll try and tell you what I mean:"

"Thank you very much," said Alice.

> "In summer, when the days are long,
> Perhaps you'll understand the song:
>
> In autumn, when the leaves are brown,
> Take pen and ink, and write it down."

"I will, if I can remember it so long," said Alice.

"You needn't go on making remarks like that," Humpty Dumpty said: "they're not sensible, and they put me out."

> "I sent a message to the fish:
> I told them 'This is what I wish.'
>
> The little fishes of the sea,
> They sent an answer back to me.
>
> The little fishes' answer was
> 'We cannot do it, Sir, because—' "

"I'm afraid I don't quite understand," said Alice.

"It gets easier further on," Humpty Dumpty replied.

"I sent to them again to say
'It will be better to obey.'

The fishes answered, with a grin,
'Why, what a temper you are in!'

I told them once, I told them twice:
They would not listen to advice.

I took a kettle large and new,
Fit for the deed I had to do.

My heart went hop, my heart went thump:
I filled the kettle at the pump.

Then some one came to me and said
'The little fishes are in bed.'

I said to him, I said it plain,
'Then you must wake them up again.'

I said it very loud and clear:
I went and shouted in his ear."

Humpty Dumpty raised his voice almost to a scream as he repeated this verse, and Alice thought, with a shudder, "I wouldn't have been the messenger for *anything*!"

"But he was very stiff and proud:
He said 'You needn't shout so loud!'

And he he was very proud and stiff:
He said 'I'd go and wake them, if—'

I took a corkscrew from the shelf:
I went to wake them up myself.

And when I found the door was locked,
I pulled and pushed and kicked and knocked.

And when I found the door was shut,
I tried to turn the handle, but—"

There was a long pause.
"Is that all?" Alice timidly asked.
"That's all," said Humpty Dumpty. "Goodbye."

THE DOZE

James Reeves

Through Dangly Woods the aimless Doze
A-dripping and a-dribbling goes.
His company no beast enjoys.
He makes a sort of hopeless noise
Between a snuffle and a snort.
His hair is neither long nor short;
His tail gets caught on briars and bushes,
As through the undergrowth he pushes.
His ears are big, but not much use.
He lives on blackberries and juice
And anything that he can get.
His feet are clumsy, wide and wet,
Slip-slopping through the bog and heather
All in the wild and weepy weather.
His young are many, and maltreat him;
But only hungry creatures eat him.
He pokes about in mossy holes,
Disturbing sleepless mice and moles,
And what he wants he never knows—
The damp, despised, and aimless Doze.

from THE WASP IN A WIG

Lewis Carroll

'' — your wig's so *very* rough, you know.''
"I'll tell you how I came to wear it," the Wasp said. "When I was young, you know, my ringlets used to wave —''

A curious idea came into Alice's head. Almost every one she had met had repeated poetry to her, and she thought she would try if the Wasp couldn't do it too. "Would you mind saying it in rhyme?'' she asked very politely.

"It aint what I'm used to," said the Wasp: "however I'll try; wait a bit." He was silent for a few moments, and then began again —

"When I was young, my ringlets waved
  And curled and crinkled on my head:
And then they said 'You should be shaved,
  And wear a yellow wig instead.'

But when I followed their advice,
  And they had noticed the effect,
They said I did not look so nice
  As they had ventured to expect.

They said it did not fit, and so
  It made me look extremely plain:
But what was I to do, you know?
  My ringlets would not grow again.

So now that I am old and gray,
  And all my hair is nearly gone,
They take my wig from me and say
  'How can you put such rubbish on?'

And still, whenever I appear,
  They hoot at me and call me 'Pig!'
And that is why they do it, dear,
  Because I wear a yellow wig."

THE PELICAN CHORUS

Edward Lear

King and Queen of the Pelicans we;
No other Birds so grand we see!
None but we have feet like fins!
With lovely leathery throats and chins!
   Ploffskin, Pluffskin, Pelican jee!
   We think no Birds so happy as we!
   Plumpskin, Ploshkin, Pelican jill!
   We think so then, and we thought so still!

We live on the Nile. The Nile we love.
By night we sleep on the cliffs above;
By day we fish, and at eve we stand
On long bare islands of yellow sand.
And when the sun sinks slowly down
And the great rock walls grow dark and brown,
Where the purple river rolls fast and dim
And the Ivory Ibis starlike skim,
Wing to wing we dance around,—
Stamping our feet with a flumpy sound,—
Opening our mouths as Pelicans ought,
And this is the song we nightly snort;—

Chorus

Last year came out our Daughter, Dell;
And all the Birds received her well.
To do her honour, a feast we made
For every bird that can swim or wade.
Herons and Gulls, and Cormorants black,
Cranes, and Flamingoes with scarlet back,
Plovers and Storks, and Geese in clouds,
Swans and Dilberry Ducks in crowds.
Thousands of Birds in wondrous flight!
They ate and drank and danced all night,
And echoing back from the rocks you heard
Multitude-echoes from Bird and Bird, —

Chorus

Yes, they came; and among the rest,
The King of the Cranes all grandly dressed.
Such a lovely tail! Its feathers float
Between the ends of his blue dress-coat;
With pea-green trowsers all so neat,
And a delicate frill to hide his feet, —
(For though no one speaks of it, every one knows,
He has got no webs between his toes!)

As soon as he saw our Daughter Dell,
In violent love that Crane King fell, —
On seeing her waddling form so fair,
With a wreath of shrimps in her short white hair.
And before the end of the next long day,
Our Dell had given her heart away;
For the King of the Cranes had won that heart,
With a Crocodile's egg and a large fish-tart.
She vowed to marry the King of the Cranes,
Leaving the Nile for stranger plains;
And away they flew in a gathering crowd
Of endless birds in a lengthening cloud.

Chorus

And far away in the twilight sky,
We heard them singing a lessening cry,—
Farther and farther till out of sight,
And we stood alone in the silent night!
Often since, in the nights of June,
We sit on the sand and watch the moon;—
She has gone to the Great Gromboolian plain,
And we probably never shall meet again!
Oft, in the long still nights of June,
We sit on the rocks and watch the moon;—
—She dwells by the streams of the Chankly Bore,
And we probably never shall see her more.

Chorus

THE WENDIGO

Ogden Nash

The Wendigo,
The Wendigo!
Its eyes are ice and indigo!
Its blood is rank and yellowish!
Its voice is hoarse and bellowish!
Its tentacles are slithery,
And scummy.
Slimy.
Leathery!
Its lips are hungry blubbery,
And smacky,
Sucky,
Rubbery!
The Wendigo,
The Wendigo!
I saw it just a friend ago!
Last night it lurked in Canada;
Tonight, on your veranada!
As you are lolling hammockwise
It contemplates you stomachwise.
You loll,
It contemplates,
It lollops.
The rest is merely gulps and gollops.

GULLIVER IN LILLIPUT

Alexander Pope

From his nose
Clouds he blows.
When he speaks,
Thunder breaks.
When he eats,
Famine threats.
When he treads.
Mountains' heads
Groan and shake;
Armies quake.
See him stride
Valleys wide,
Over woods,
Over floods.
Troops take heed,
Man and steed:
Left and right.
Speed your flight!
In amaze
Lost I gaze
Toward the skies:
See! and believe your eyes!

CHILD'S GAME

Alan Riddell

```
hide-and-seek
 hideand-seek
  hidand-seek
   hidnd-seek
    hadd-seek
   hidnd-seek
  hidand-seek
 hideand-seek
hide-and-seek
hide-andseek
hide-andeek
hide-andek
hide-andk
hide-andek
hide-andeek
hide-andseek
hide-and-seek
```

COLONEL FAZACKERLEY

Charles Causley

Colonel Fazackerley Butterworth-Toast
Bought an old castle complete with a ghost,
But someone or other forgot to declare
To Colonel Fazack that the spectre was there.

On the very first evening, while waiting to dine,
The Colonel was taking a fine sherry wine,
When the ghost with a furious flash and a flare,
Shot out of the chimney and shivered, 'Beware!'

Colonel Fazackerley put down his glass
And said, 'My dear fellow, that's really first class!
I just can't conceive how you do it at all,
I imagine you're going to a Fancy Dress Ball?'

At this, the dread ghost gave a withering cry.
Said the Colonel (his monocle firm in his eye),
'Now just how you do it I wish I could think.
Do sit down and tell me, and please have a drink.'

The ghost in his phosphorous cloak gave a roar
And floated about between ceiling and floor.
He walked through a wall and returned through a pane
And backed up the chimney and came down again.

Said the Colonel, 'With laughter I'm feeling quite weak!'
(As trickles of merriment ran down his cheek).
'My house-warming party I hope you won't spurn.
You must say you'll come and you'll give us a turn!'

At this the poor spectre — quite out of his wits —
Proceeded to shake himself almost to bits.
He rattled his chains and he clattered his bones
And he filled the whole castle with mumbles and moans.

But Colonel Fazackerley, just as before,
Was simply delighted and called out, 'Encore!'
At which the ghost vanished, his efforts in vain,
And never was seen at the castle again.

'Oh dear, what a pity!' said Colonel Fazack.
'I don't know his name, so I can't call him back.'
And then with a smile that was hard to define,
Colonel Fazackerley went in to dine.

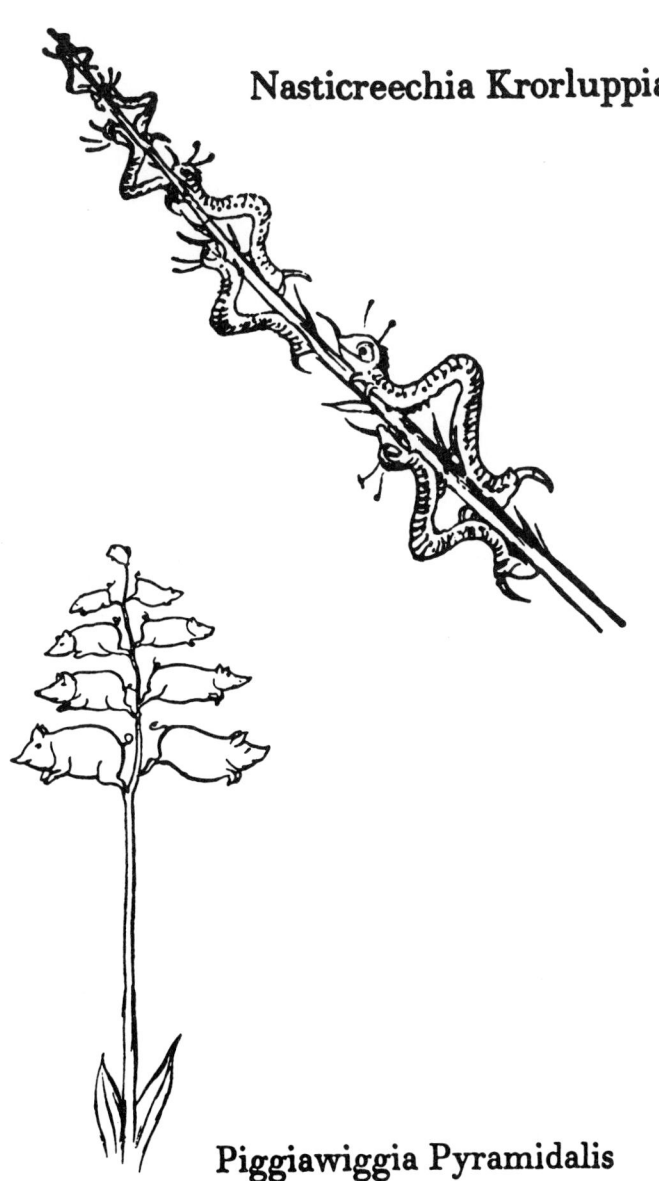

Nasticreechia Krorluppia

Piggiawiggia Pyramidalis

THE GREAT PANJANDRUM

Samuel Foote

So she went into the garden
to cut a cabbage-leaf
to make an apple-pie;
and at the same time
a great she-bear, coming down the street,
pops its head into the shop. What! no soap?
   So he died,
and she very imprudently married the Barber:
and there were present
the Picninnies,
    and the Joblillies,
      and the Garyulies,
and the great Panjandrum himself,
with the little round button at top;
and they all fell to playing the game of catch-as-catch-can,
till the gunpowder ran out at the heels of their boots.

Talking and Writing

Manypeeplia Upsidownia

— Alice is disappointed because Humpty Dumpty's poem on page 38 finishes so suddenly. What do you think happens next? Can you write some more rhyming lines to continue the story?

— *The Pelican Chorus* on page 42 is a good poem to read aloud in groups or all together. Perhaps you could make a tape recording with different groups reading out different parts of the poem. When you know it well, you may be able to bring in the music.

—*The Doze* on page 40 and *The Wendigo* on page 44 are two imaginary creatures. Invent your own monster, draw it, give it a name and write about it.

— Can you invent your own plants like those in the *Nonsense Botany* on pages 47 and 48? Use everyday objects to make up the flowers, draw them, give them a name, and write about where they are found and how they are used.

Phattfacia Stupenda

Looking
and Seeing

RIDDLE

Kevin Crossley-Holland

My breast is puffed up and my neck is swollen.
I've a fine head and a high waving tail,
ears and eyes also but only one foot;
a long neck, a strong beak, a back and
two sides, and a rod right through my middle.
My home is high above men. When he who moves
the forest molests me, I suffer a great deal of misery.
Scourged by the rainlash, I stand alone;
I'm bruised by heavy batteries of hail,
Hoar frost attacks and snow half-hides me.
I must endure all this, not pour out my misery.

RIDDLES

from The Hobbit by J.R.R. Tolkien

Thirty white horses on a red hill,
   First they champ,
   Then they stamp,
Then they stand still.

Voiceless it cries,
Wingless flutters,
Toothless bites,
Mouthless mutters.

Alive without breath,
As cold as death;
Never thirsty, ever drinking,
All in mail never clinking.

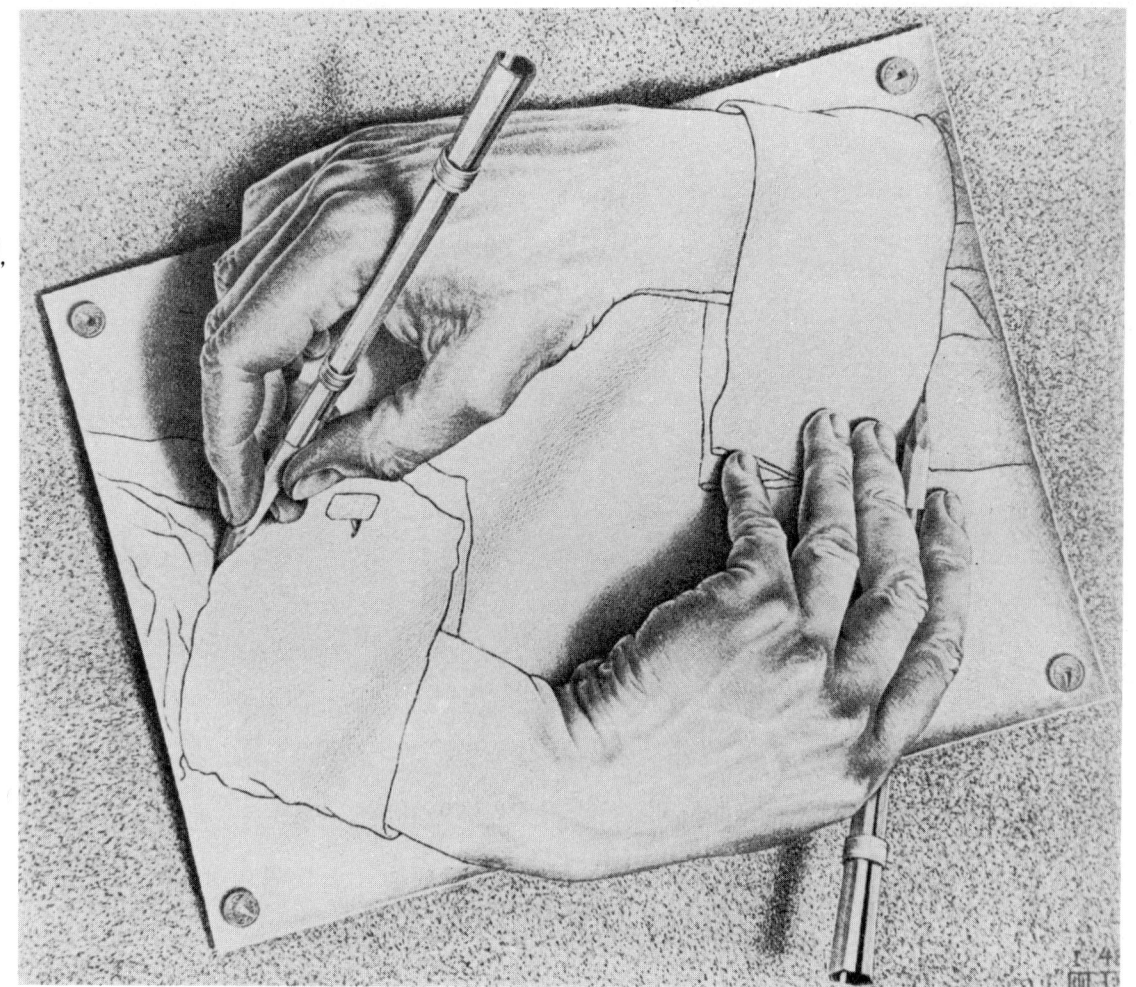

HIDE AND SEEK

Walter De la Mare

Hide and seek, says the Wind,
  In the shade of the woods;
Hide and seek, says the Moon,
  To the hazel buds;
Hide and seek, says the Cloud,
  Star on to star;
Hide and seek, says the Wave
  At the harbour bar;
Hide and seek, say I,
  To myself, and step
Out of the dream of Wake
  Into the dream of Sleep.

THE TIDE IN THE RIVER

Eleanor Farjeon

The tide in the river,
  The tide in the river,
The tide in the river runs deep,
  I saw a shiver
  Pass over the river
As the tide turned in its sleep.

BUTTERFLIES

Chu Miao Tuan

(TRANS. HENRY H. HART)

The blossoms fall like snowflakes
On the cool, deep, dark-green moss,
They lie in white-heaped fragrant drifts
Before the courtyard gates.

The butterflies, not knowing
That the days of spring are done,
Still pursue the flying petals
Across the garden wall.

THE SNOWFLAKE

Walter De la Mare

Before I melt,
Come, look at me!
This lovely ice filigree!
Of a great forest
In one night!
I make a wilderness
Of white:
By skyey cold
Of crystals made.
All softly, on
Your finger laid,
I pause, that you
My beauty see:
Breathe, and I vanish
Instantly.

SEEDS

Walter De la Mare

The seeds I sowed —
For weeks unseen —
Have pushed up pygmy
Shoots of green;
So frail you'd think
The tiniest stone
Would never let
A glimpse be shown.
But no, a pebble
Near them lies,
At least a cherry-stone
In size,
Which that mere sprout
Has heaved away,
To bask in sunshine,
See the day.

Cat

Keith Bosley

Cat
purring

four furry paws
walking

delicate-
ly
    between
flower stems
stalking

butter-
flies

'MY DAD'S THUMB'

Michael Rosen

My dad's thumb
can stick pins in wood
without flinching —
it can crush family-size matchboxes
in one stroke
and lever off jam-jar lids without piercing
at the pierce here sign.

If it wanted
it could be a bath-plug
or a paint-scraper
a keyhole cover or a tap-tightener.

It's already a great nutcracker
and if it dressed up
it could easily pass
as a broad bean or a big toe.

In actual fact, it's quite simply
the world's fastest envelope burster.

INTRUDER

Clive Sansom

The sun only scorches,
It doesn't watch; but the moon watches.
He peers down low at the earth
As we cross his path;
He fills the unmoving meadows
With white light and dark moon-shadows;
He stares into my room as far as he can reach,
Like a man with a large torch.

Talking and Writing

— Making up riddles is an ancient game. Some we know about are more than two thousand years old. The one on page 50 is more than a thousand years old from a time when people used to be very fond of riddling competitions. You may know the riddles from *The Hobbit* on page 51.

Read through the riddles and try to work out what they describe. (*The answers are on page 96*).

Can you make up a riddle to describe an everyday object like a ruler, a pencil, a pair of compasses?

— We look at things all the time but we do not always see details as clearly as we might. The poems on page 53 are about things observed very closely. Choose a familiar object: a leaf, a flower, a stone, a piece of bark . . .

What does it look like?
What does it feel like?
What does it remind you of?

Write your description in as much detail as you can.

— People say they know things like the back of their hand. How well do you know *your* hand? Is it at all like the hands in the picture on page 51. Look carefully at your own hand and try to describe it in detail. You may find it helpful to make a hand-print.

— Walter De la Mare's poem *Hide and Seek* is about the time when we are lying in bed, half awake and half asleep. Imagine yourself in this state. What sort of pictures are in your mind's eye? What sounds are you aware of? What stories or day-dreams do you invent?

Try to write a description with either the title 'Falling Asleep' or 'Coming Awake'.

People
and Places

TELEVISION

Roald Dahl
from *Charlie and the Chocolate Factory*

The most important thing we've learned,
So far as children are concerned,
Is never, *never*, NEVER let
Them near your television set —
Or better still, just don't install
The idiotic thing at all.
In almost every house we've been,
We've watched them gaping at the screen,
They loll and slop and lounge about,
And stare until their eyes pop out.
(Last week in someone's place we saw
A dozen eyeballs on the floor.)
They sit and stare and stare and sit
Until they're hypnotised by it,
Until they're absolutely drunk
With all that shocking ghastly junk.
Oh yes, we know it keeps them still,
They don't climb out the window sill,
They never fight or kick or punch,
They leave you free to cook the lunch
And wash the dishes in the sink —
But did you ever stop to think,
To wonder just exactly what
This does to your beloved tot?

IT ROTS THE SENSES IN THE HEAD!
IT KILLS IMAGINATION DEAD!
IT CLOGS AND CLUTTERS UP THE MIND!
IT MAKES A CHILD SO DULL AND BLIND
HE CAN NO LONGER UNDERSTAND
A FANTASY: A FAIRYLAND!
HIS BRAIN BECOMES AS SOFT AS CHEESE!
HIS POWERS OF THINKING RUST AND FREEZE!
HE CANNOT THINK — HE ONLY SEES!

"All right!" you'll cry. "All right!" you'll say,
"But if we take the set away,
What shall we do to entertain
Our darling children! Please explain!"
We'll answer this by asking you,
"What used the darling ones to do?
How used they keep themselves contented
Before this monster was invented?"
Have you forgotten? Don't you know?
We'll say it very loud and slow:

THEY. . .USED. . . TO . . . READ! They'd READ and READ,
AND READ and READ, and then proceed
To READ some more. Great Scott! Gadzooks!
One half their lives was reading books!
The nursery shelves held books galore!
Books cluttered up the nursery floor!
And in the bedroom, by the bed,
More books were waiting to be read!
Such wondrous, fine, fantastic tales
Of dragons, gypsies, queens and whales
And treasure isles, and distant shores

Where smugglers rowed with muffled oars,
And pirates wearing purple pants,
And sailing ships and elephants,
And cannibals crouching round the pot,
Stirring away at something hot.
(It smells so good, what can it be?
Good gracious, it's Penelope.)
The younger ones had Beatrix Potter
With Mr Todd, the dirty rotter,
And Squirrel Nutkin, Pigling Bland,
And Mrs Tiggy-Winkle and —
Just How The Camel Got his Hump,
And How The Monkey Lost His Rump,
And Mr Toad, and bless my soul,
There's Mr Rat and Mr Mole —
Oh, books, what books they used to know,
Those children living long ago!
So please, oh *please*, we beg, we pray,
Go throw your TV set away.

And in its place you can install
A lovely bookshelf on the wall.
Then fill the shelves with lots of books,
Ignoring all the dirty looks,
The screams and yells, the bites and kicks,
And children hitting you with sticks —
Fear not, because we promise you
That, in about a week or two
Of having nothing else to do,
They'll now begin to feel the need
Of having something good to read,
And once they start — oh boy, oh boy!
You watch the slowly growing joy

That fills their hearts. They'll grow so keen
They'll wonder what they'd ever seen
In that ridiculous machine.
That nauseating, foul, unclean,
Repulsive television screen!
And later, each and every kid
Will love you more for what you did.

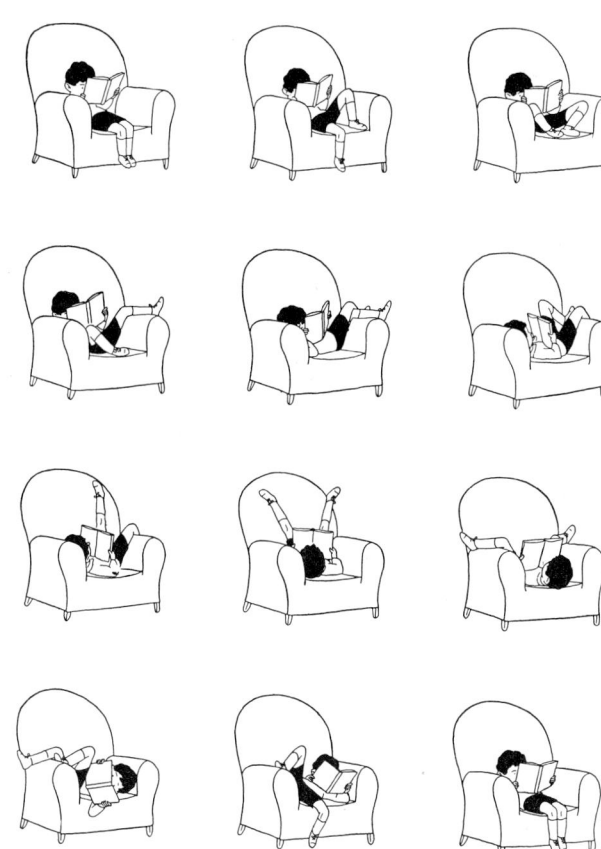

THE CAMEL'S HUMP

Rudyard Kipling

The Camel's hump is an ugly hump
  Which well you may see at the Zoo;
But uglier yet is the hump we get
  From having too little to do.

Kiddies and grown-up too-oo-oo,
If we haven't enough to do-oo-oo,
  We get the hump—
  Cameelious hump—
The hump that is black and blue

We climb out of bed with a frouzly head
  And a snarly-yarly voice.
We shiver and scowl and we grunt and we growl
  At our bath and our boots and our toys;

And there ought to be a corner for me
(And I know there is one for you)
  When we get the hump—
  Cameelious hump—
The hump that is black and blue!

The cure for this ill is not to sit still,
  Or frowst with a book by the fire;
But to take a large hoe and a shovel also,
  And dig till you gently perspire;

And then you will find that the sun and the wind,
And the Djinn of the Garden too,
  Have lifted the hump—
  The horrible hump—
The hump that is black and blue!

I get it as well as you-oo-oo—
If I haven't enough to do-oo-oo!
  We all get hump—
  Cameelious hump—
Kiddies and grown-ups too!

THREE JOLLY HUNTSMEN

Anon

Three jolly huntsmen,
I've heard people say,
Went hunting together
On St. David's Day.

All day they hunted,
And nothing could they find,
But a ship a-sailing,
A-sailing with the wind.

One said it was a ship,
The other he said, Nay;
The third said it was a house,
With the chimney blown away.

And all the night they hunted,
And nothing could they find
But the moon a-gliding,
A-gliding with the wind.

One said it was the moon,
The other he said, Nay;
The third said it was a cheese,
And half of it cut away.

And all the day they hunted,
And nothing did they find
But a hedgehog in a bramble-bush,
And that they left behind.

The first said it was a hedgehog,
The second he said, Nay;
The third said it was a pin cushion,
And the pins stuck in wrong way.

And all the night they hunted,
And nothing could they find
But a hare in a turnip-field,
And that they left behind.

The first said it was a hare,
The second he said, Nay;
The third said it was a calf,
And the cow had run away.

And all the day they hunted,
And nothing could they find
But an owl in a holly-tree,
And that they left behind.

One said it was an owl,
The second he said, Nay;
The third said 'twas an old man,
And his beard was growing gray.

THE OLD SAILOR

Walter De la Mare

There came an old sailor
Who sat to sup
Under the trees
Of the Golden Cup.

Beer in a mug
And a slice of cheese
With a hunk of bread
He munched at his ease.

Then in the summer
Dusk he lit
A little black pipe.
And sucked at it.

He thought of his victuals.
Of Ships, the sea.
Of his home in the West,
And his children three.

And he stared and stared
To where, afar,
The lighthouse gleamed
At the harbour bar;

Till his pipe grew cold,
And down on the board
He laid his head,
And snored, snored, snored.

MISS T.

Walter De la Mare

OLD PEOPLE

Elizabeth Jennings

Why are people impatient when they are old?
Is it because they are tired of trying to make
Fast things move slowly?
I have seen their eyes flinch as they watch the lorries
Lurching and hurrying past.
I have also seen them twitch and move away
When a grandbaby cries.
They can go to the cinema cheaply.
They can do what they like all day.
Yet they shrink and shiver, looking like old, used dolls.
I do not think that I should like to be old.

It's a very odd thing —
  As odd as can be —
That whatever Miss T. eats
  Turns into Miss T.;
Porridge and apples,
  Mince, muffins, and mutton,
Jam, junket, jumbles —
  Not a rap, not a button
It matters; the moment
  They're out of her plate,
Though shared by Miss Butcher
  And sour Mr Bate;
Tiny and cheerful,
  And neat as can be,
Whatever Miss T. eats
Turns into Miss T.

DUSTMAN

Clive Sansom

Every Thursday morning
Before we're quite awake,
Without the slightest warning
The house begins to shake
    With a Biff! Bang!
    Biff! Bang! Biff!
It's the Dustman, who begins
    (BANG! CRASH!)
To empty all the bins
Of their rubbish and their ash
    With a Biff! Bang!
    Biff! Bang! Crash!

A TRANSPORT OF DELIGHT
(THE OMNIBUS)

Michael Flanders and
Donald Swann

Some talk of a Lagonda,
Some like a smart M.G.,
Or for Bonnie Army Lorry
They'd lay them doon and dee.
Such means of locomotion
Seem rather dull to us—
The Driver and Conductor
Of a London Omnibus.

Hold very tight please, ting-ting!

When you are lost in London
And you don't know where you are,
You'll hear my voice a-calling:
'Pass further down the car!'
And very soon you'll find yourself
Inside the Terminus
   In a London Transport
   Diesel-engined
   Ninety-seven horse-power
   Omnibus!

Along the Queen's great highway
I drive my merry load
At twenty miles per hour
In the middle of the road;
We like to drive in convoys—
We're most gregarious;
   The big six-wheeler
   Scarlet-painted
   London Transport
   Diesel-engined
   Ninety-seven horse-power
   Omnibus!

Earth has not anything to show more fair!
Mind the stairs! Mind the stairs!
Earth has not anything to show more fair!
Any more fares? Any more fares?

When cabbies try to pass me,
Before they overtakes,
I sticks me flippin' hand out
As I jams on all me brakes!
Them jackal taxi-drivers
Can only swear and cuss,
   Behind that monarch of the road,
   Observer of the Highway Code,
   That big six-wheeler
   Scarlet-painted
   London Transport
   Diesel-engined
   Ninety-seven horse-power
   Omnibus!

I stops when I'm requested
Although it spoils the ride,
So he can shout: 'Get aht of it!
We're full right up inside!'

We don't ask much for wages,
We only want fair shares,
So cut down all the stages,
And stick up all the fares.
If tickets cost a pound apiece
Why should you make a fuss?
It's worth it just ride inside
That thirty-foot-long by ten-foot-wide
   Inside that monarch of the road,
   Observer of the Highway Code,
   That big six-wheeler
   Scarlet-painted
   London Transport
   Diesel-engined
   Ninety-seven horse-power
   Omnibus!

OLD MRS THING-UM-E-BOB

Charles Causley

Old Mrs Thing-um-e-bob,
  Lives at you-know-where.
Dropped her what-you-may-call-it down
  The well of the kitchen stair.

'Gracious me!' said Thing-um-e-bob,
  'This don't look too bright.
I'll ask old Mr What's-his-name
  To try to put it right.'

Along came Mr What's-his-name,
  He said, 'You've broke the lot!
I'll have to see what I can do
  With some of the you-know-what.'

So he gave the what-you-may-call-it a pit
  And he gave it a bit of a pat,
And he put it all together again
  With a little of this and that.

And he gave the what-you-may-call-it a dib
  And he gave it a dab as well
When all of a sudden he heard a note
  As clear as any bell.

It's as good as new!' cried What's-his-name.
  'But please remember, now,
In future Mrs Thing-um-e-bob
  You'll have to go you-know-how.'

Talking and Writing

— The bus driver in the poem on page 64 seems to enjoy his job. What sort of job would you like to do? Can you write about it?

Read the poem about the dustman on page 63. Think of the people you often see — the postman, the milk-man, shopkeepers or the people at the supermarket. Try to write a really vivid description of one of them.

— 'I do not think I should like to be old,' says Elizabeth Jennings at the end of her poem on page 62. Would you like to be old? Are there any good things about being old?

If you know an old person perhaps you could write about him or her. Put one idea on each line and try to say what the person looks like, how the person moves, what his voice is like, the kind of thing he says and anything else that will help to give a picture.

— Just about all the people in Hervey Street came out for the photograph on page 63. Look closely at the picture and try to guess about the people in it. What are they like? What do you imagine they do?

Can you write about the people who live in your own street?

— All of us become fed-up from time to time through being bored. The poem on page 60 tells us one way to get over it.

Can you describe your feelings when *you* are bored? Are there any special things that make you fed up? What do you do to shake off this mood?

— Is T.V. "the monster" that Roald Dahl describes on page 58 or do you think of it as a more friendly animal?

Draw your own T.V. creature. It might be a monstrous beast that lives on children's eyeballs or a domestic pet that you enjoy living with. Give your creature a name and try to write about it.

Stories

OFF THE GROUND

Walter De la Mare

Three jolly Farmers
Once bet a pound
Each dance the others would
Off the ground.

Out of their coats
They slipped right soon,
And neat and nicesome,
Put each his shoon.

One — Two — Three! —
And away they go,
Not too fast,
And not too slow:
Out from the elm-tree's
Noonday shadow,
Into the sun
And across the meadow.
Past the schoolroom,
With knees well bent
Fingers a-flicking,
They dancing went.
Up sides and over,
And round and round,
They crossed click-clacking,
The Parish bound.

By Tupman's meadow
They did their mile,
Tee-to-tum
On a three-barred stile.
Then straight through Whipham,
Downhill to Week,
Footing it lightsome,
But not too quick,
Up fields to Watchet,
And on through Wye,
Till seven fine churches
They'd seen skip by —
Seven fine churches,
And five old mills,
Farms in the valley,
And sheep on the hills;
Old Man's Acre
And Dead Man's Pool
All left behind,
As they danced through Wool.

And Wool gone by,
Like tops that seem
To spin in sleep
They danced in dream:
Withy — Wellover —
Wassop — Wo —
Like an old clock
Their heels did go.
A league and a league
And a league they went,

And not one weary,
And not one spent.
And lo, and behold!
Past Willow-cum-Leigh
Stretched with its waters
The great green sea.

Says Farmer Bates,
'I puffs and I blows,
What's under the water,
Why, no man knows!'
Says Farmer Giles,
'My wind comes weak,
And a good man drownded
Is far to seek'.
But Farmer Turvey,
On twirling toes
Up's with his gaiters,
And in he goes:
Down where the mermaids
Pluck and play
On their twangling harps
In a sea-green day;
Down where the mermaids,
Finned and fair,
Sleek with their combs
Their yellow hair . . . .

Bates and Giles —
On the shingle sat,
Gazing at Turvey's

Floating hat.
But never a ripple
Nor bubble told
Where he was supping
Off plates of gold.
Never an echo
Rilled through the sea
Of the feasting and dancing
And minstrelsy.
They called — called — called:
Came no reply:
Nought but the ripples'
Sandy sigh.

Then glum and silent
They sat instead,
Vacantly brooding
On home and bed,
Till both together
Stood up and said:-
'Us knows not, dreams not,
Where you be,
Turvey, unless
In the deep blue sea;
But axcusing silver —
And it comes most willing —
Here's us two paying
Our forty shilling;
For it's sartin sure, Turvey,
Safe and sound,
You danced us square, Turvey;
Off the ground!'

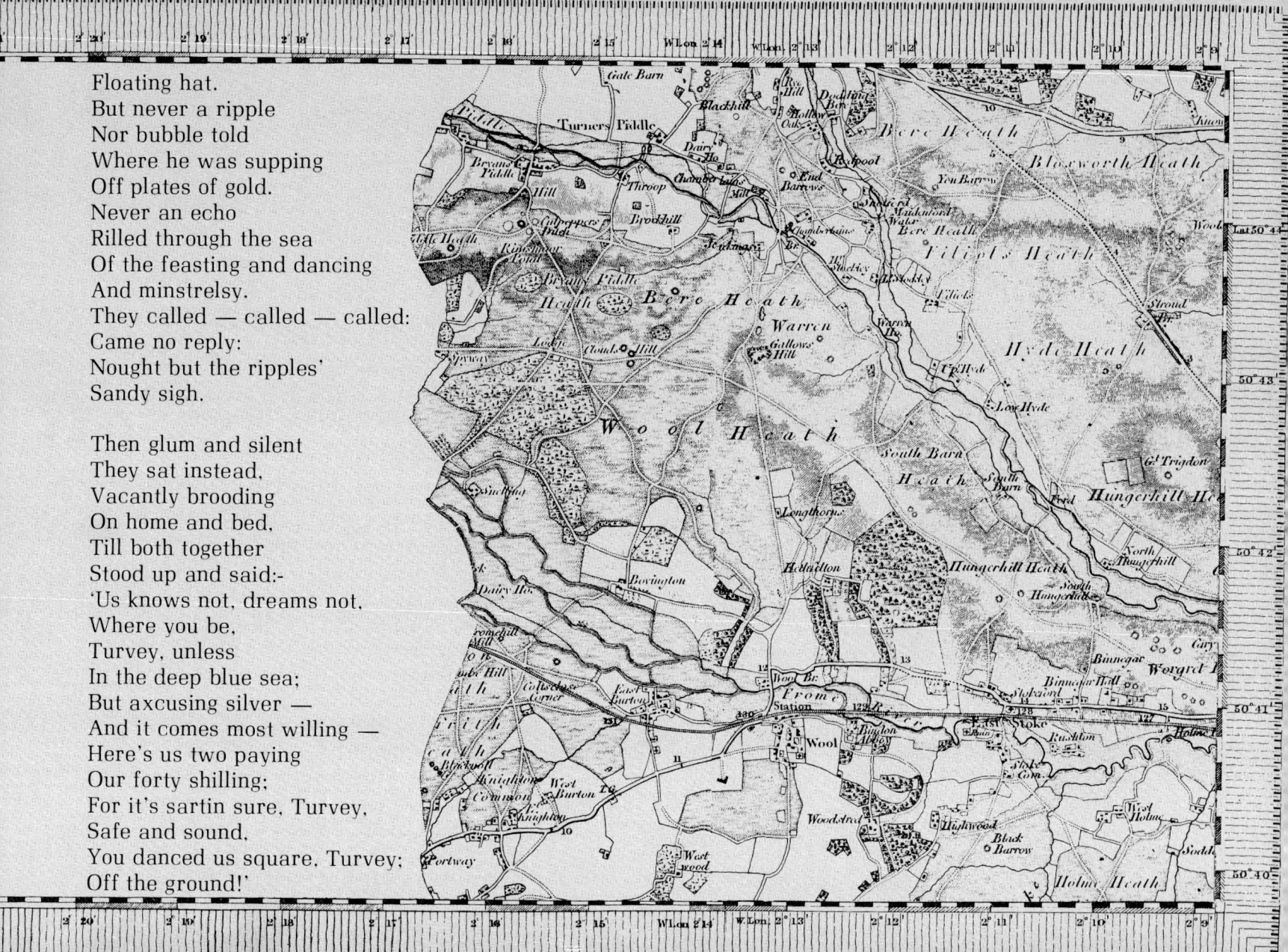

THE RESCUE

Hal Summers

The boy climbed up into the tree.
The tree rocked. So did he.
He was trying to rescue a cat,
A cushion of a cat, from where it sat
In a high crutch of branches, mewing
As though to say to him, 'Nothing doing,'
Whenever he shouted, 'Come on, come down,'
So up he climbed, and the whole town
Lay at his feet, round him the leaves
Fluttered like a lady's sleeves,
And the cat sat, and the wind blew so
That he would have flown had he let go.

At last he was high enough to scoop
That fat white cushion or nincompoop
And tuck her under his arm and turn
To go down—
        But oh! he began to learn
How high he was, how hard it would be,
Having come up with four limbs, to go down with three.
His heart-beats knocked as he tried to think:
He would put the cat in a lower chink—
She appealed to him with a cry of alarm
And put her eighteen claws in his arm.
So he stayed looking down for a minute or so,
To the good ground so far below.
When the minute began he saw it was hard;
When it ended he couldn't move a yard.
So there he was stuck, in the failing light
And the wind rising with the coming of the night.

His father! He shouted for all he was worth.
His father came nearer: 'What on earth—?'

'I've got the cat up here but I'm stuck.'
'Hold on . . . ladder . . .', he heard. O luck!
How lovely behind the branches tossing
The globes at the pedestrian crossing
And the big fluorescent lamps glowed
Mauve-green on the main road.
But his father didn't come back, didn't come;
His little fingers were going numb.
The cat licked them as though to say
'Are you feeling cold? I'm O.K.'

He wanted to cry, he would count ten first,
But just as he was ready to burst
A torch came and his father and mother
And a ladder and the dog and his younger brother.
Up on a big branch stood his father,
His mother came to the top of the ladder,
His brother stood on a lower rung,
The dog sat still and put out its tongue
From one to the other the cat was handed
And afterwards she was reprimanded.
After that it was easy, though the wind blew:
The parents came down, the boy came too
From the ladder, the lower branch and the upper
And all of them went indoors to supper,
And the tree rocked, and the moon sat
In the high branches like a white cat.

THE CRANE AND THE BONE OF CONTENTION

Brian Patten

The wolf, a most amazing glutton,
One day nearly choked on mutton.
In his throat a large bone stuck
But, by a stroke of luck,
A crane passing and looking round
For anything that might be about,
Heard a funny kind of shout.

'Gelp! cane, gum gere:
Get gis gone gout gy groat!'

Always ready to help a wolf in need
The crane went to the creature's aid,
And hoping she would be well paid
Soon on the ground the bone was laid.
The bird then asked for her fee.
'Why, of course!' was the wolf's reply.

It grabbed the crane by the throat
And then let go when the crane cried out,
'I've helped you, so now spare my life!'
'Why of course,' said the wolf, 'and life is your fee
For all the help you have given me.'

THE LION'S WORST ENEMY

Brian Patten

The king of all beasts deep in the wood
Roared as loudly as it could.
And when from a cave the echo came back
The lion thought itself under attack.

'What voice is that that roars like mine?'
The echo replied, 'Mine, mine.'

'Who might you be?' asked the furious lion;
'I am king of this jungle, this jungle is mine!'
And the echo came back for a third time,
'This jungle is mine, is mine, is mine.'

The lion swore it would murder its enemy if it only could
Discover its whereabouts in that deep wood.
It roared, 'Mimic, come out and show yourself!'
But the fearless echo replied simply, 'Elf.'

'Come out,' roared the lion, 'Enough deceit —
Do you fear for your own defeat?'
But all the echo did was repeat
The cankerous word, 'Defeat, defeat . . .'

Frightened by every conceivable sound
The exhausted lion sank to the ground.
A bird in a tree looked down and it said,
'Sweet beast, I'm afraid what you hear
Is simply the voice of your lion-sized fear.'

GREEN MAN IN THE GARDEN

Charles Causley

Green man in the garden
 Staring from the tree,
Why do you look so long and hard
 Through the pane at me?

Your eyes are dark as holly,
 Of sycamore your horns,
Your bones are made of elder-branch,
 Your teeth are made of thorns.

Your hat is made of ivy-leaf,
 Of bark your dancing shoes,
And evergreen and green and green
 Your jacket and shirt and trews.

Leave your house and leave your land
 And throw away the key,
And never look behind, he creaked,
 And come and live with me.

I bolted up the window,
 I bolted up the door,
I drew the blind that I should find
 The green man never more.

But when I softly turned the stair
 As I went up to bed,
I saw the green man standing there.
 Sleep well, my friend, he said.

THE MAGIC WOOD

Henry Treece

The wood is full of shining eyes,
The wood is full of creeping feet,
The wood is full of tiny cries:
You must not go to the wood at night!

I met a man with eyes of glass
And a finger as curled as the wriggling worm,
And hair all red with rotting leaves,
And a stick that hissed like a summer snake.

The wood is full of shining eyes,
The wood is full of creeping feet,
The wood is full of tiny cries:
You must not go to the wood at night!

He sang me a song in backwards words,
And drew me a dragon in the air.
I saw his teeth through the back of his head,
And a rat's eyes winking from his hair.

The wood is full of shining eyes,
The wood is full of creeping feet,
The wood is full of tiny cries:
You must not go to the wood at night!

He made me a penny out of a stone,
And showed me the way to catch a lark
With a straw and a nut and a whispered word
And a pennorth of ginger wrapped up in a leaf.

The wood is full of shining eyes,
The wood is full of creeping feet,
The wood is full of tiny cries:
You must not go to the wood at night!

He asked me my name, and where I lived;
I told him a name from my Book of Tales;
He asked me to come with him into the wood
And dance with the Kings from under the hills.

The wood is full of shining eyes,
The wood is full of creeping feet,
The wood is full of tiny cries:
You must not go to the wood at night!

But I saw that his eyes were turning to fire;
I watched the nails grow on his wriggling hand;
And I said my prayers, all out in a rush,
And found myself safe on my father's land.

Oh, the wood is full of shining eyes,
The wood is full of creeping feet,
The wood is full of tiny cries:
You must not go to the wood at night!

THE SPIDER

Michael Flanders and
Donald Swann

I have fought a grizzly bear,
Tracked a cobra to its lair,
Killed a crocodile who dared to cross my path;
But the thing I really dread
When I've just got out of bed
Is to find that there's a spider in the bath.

I've no fear of wasps or bees,
Mosquitos only tease,
I rather like a cricket on the hearth;
But my blood runs cold to meet
In pyjamas and bare feet
With a great big hairy spider in the bath.

I have faced a charging bull in Barcelona,
I have dragged a mountain lioness from her cub,
I've restored a mad gorilla to its owner
But I don't dare to face that Tub . . .

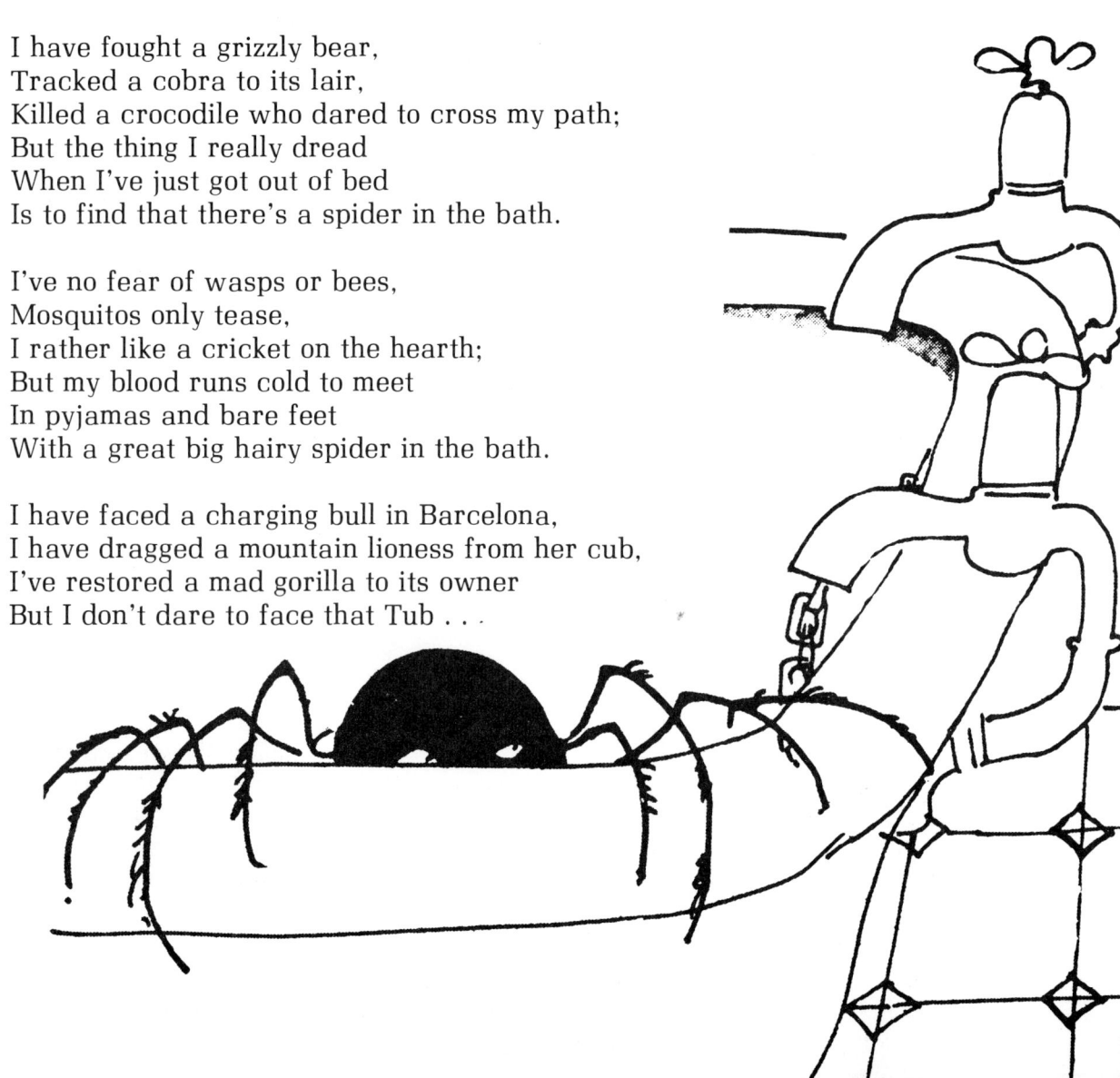

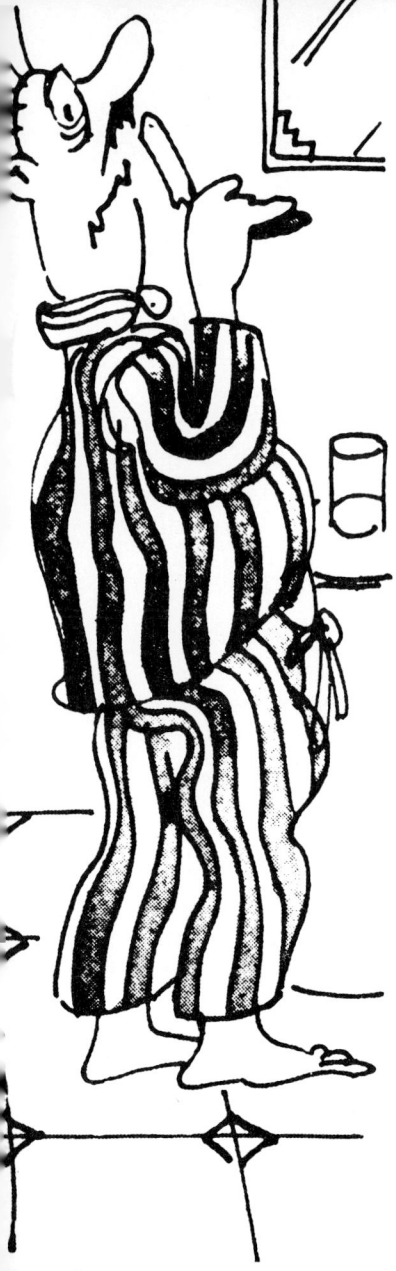

What a frightful-looking beast—
Half an inch across at least—
It would frighten even Superman or Garth.
There's contempt it can't disguise
In the little beady eyes
Of the spider sitting glowering in the bath.

It ignores my every lunge
With the back-brush and the sponge;
I have bombed it with 'A Present from Penarth';
But it doesn't mind at all—
It just rolls into a ball
And simply goes on squatting in the bath . . .

For hours we have been locked in endless struggle;
I have lured it to the deep end, by the drain;
At last I think I've washed it down the plug-'ole
But here it comes a-crawling up the chain!

Now it's time for me to shave
Though my nerves will not behave,
And there's bound to be a fearful aftermath;
So before I cut my throat
I shall leave this final note:
DRIVEN TO IT — BY THE SPIDER IN THE BATH!

FIGGIE HOBBIN

Charles Causley

Nightingales' tongues, your majesty?
    Quails in aspic, cost a purse of money?
Oysters from the deep, raving sea?
    Grapes and Greek honey?
Beads of black caviare from the Caspian?
    Rock melon with corn on the cob in?
Take it all away! grumbled the old King of Cornwall.
    Bring me some figgie hobbin!

Devilled lobster, your majesty?
    Scots kail brose or broth?
Grilled mackerel with gooseberry sauce?
    Cider ice that melts in your mouth?
Pears filled with nut and date salad?
    Christmas pudding with a tanner or a bob in?
Take it all away! groused the old King of Cornwall.
    Bring me some figgie hobbin!

Amber jelly, your majesty?
    Passion fruit flummery?
Pineapple sherbet, milk punch or Pavlova cake,
    Sugary, summery?
Carpet-bag steak, blueberry grunt, cinnamon crescents?
    Spaghetti as fine as the thread on a bobbin?
Take it all away! grizzled the old King of Cornwall.
    Bring me some figgie hobbin!

So in from the kitchen came figgie hobbin,
    Shining and speckled with raisins sweet,
And though on the King of Cornwall's land
    The rain it fell and the wind it beat,
As soon as a forkful of figgie hobbin
    Up to his lips he drew,
Over the palace a pure sun shone
    And the sky was blue.
THAT'S what I wanted! he smiled, his face
    Now as bright as the breast of the robin.
To cure the sickness of the heart, ah—
    Bring me some figgie hobbin!

FIGGIE HOBBIN – Recipe

½lb plain flour
¾-teaspoon baking powder
2oz chopped suet
2oz lard
½lb dried chopped figs
2-3 fl oz milk
Oven 400°F gas mark 6 – for 30 minutes

Sift flour and baking powder, rub in the suet and lard and mix with the chopped figs. Blend in enough milk to give a stiff dough. Roll dough out to half-inch thick on a floured surface and cut into 4 inch squares. Set on greased baking trays, score the surface lightly and bake.

Talking and Writing

— If you make up your own story you usually have some idea about what is going to happen and how it will end; but a story made up by the whole class could end anywhere . . . . Try it and see. One of you, perhaps your teacher, invents the first line and then everybody adds a sentence in turn.

You might like to try this first as a spoken story. A written story could be made up in the same way, either on paper or on the blackboard.

— There is a lively, dancing rhythm to the poem *Off the Ground* on page 68. In groups of three, can you mime the journey of the three farmers? It might help to pick out the rhythm on a percussion instrument or a piano.

— There are many fables about animals like the one on page 72 about the fox and the crane. What sort of story is a fable? Do you know any others?

Can you make up your own fable about two (or more) animals? The picture of the owl and the rat opposite or the picture on page 73 might give you an idea for starting.

— There is something strange and frightening about the *Green Man In the Garden* on page 74 and the man in *The Magic Wood* on page 75. Can you draw one of them?

Now invent your own frightening person, draw a picture of him and write about what he looks like and what he does.

Creatures

GROWLTIGER'S LAST STAND

T. S. Eliot

Growltiger was a Bravo Cat, who travelled on a barge:
In fact he was the roughest cat that ever roamed at large.
From Gravesend up to Oxford he pursued his evil aims,
Rejoicing in his title of 'The Terror of the Thames'.

His manners and appearance did not calculate to please;
His coat was torn and seedy, he was baggy at the knees;
One ear was somewhat missing, no need to tell you why,
And he scowled upon a hostile world from one forbidding ey

The cottagers of Rotherhithe knew something of his fame;
At Hammersmith and Putney people shuddered at his name.
They would fortify the hen-house, lock up the silly goose,
When the rumour ran along the shore: GROWLTIGER'S ON
    THE LOOSE!

Woe to the weak canary, that fluttered from its cage;
Woe to the pampered Pekinese, that faced Growltiger's rage;
Woe to the bristly Bandicoot, that lurks on foreign ships,
And woe to any Cat with whom Growltiger came to grips!

ut most to Cats of foreign race his hatred had been vowed;
o Cats of foreign name and race no quarter was allowed.
he Persian and the Siamese regarded him with fear—
ecause it was a Siamese had mauled his missing ear.

ow on a peaceful summer night, all nature seemed at play,
he tender moon was shining bright, the barge at Molesey lay,
ll in the balmy moonlight it lay rocking on the tide—
nd Growltiger was disposed to show his sentimental side.

lis bucko mate, GRUMBUSKIN, long since had disappeared,
or to the Bell at Hampton he had gone to wet his beard;
nd his bosun, TUMBLEBRUTUS, he too had stol'n away—
1 the yard behind the Lion he was prowling for his prey.

1 the forepeak of the vessel Growltiger sat alone,
oncentrating his attention on the Lady GRIDDLEBONE.
nd his raffish crew were sleeping in their barrels and their bunks—
s the Siamese came creeping in their sampans and their junks.

rowltiger had no eye or ear for aught but Griddlebone,
nd the Lady seemed enraptured by his manly baritone,
isposed to relaxation, and awaiting no surprise—
ut the moonlight shone reflected from a hundred bright blue eyes.

nd closer still and closer the sampans circled round,
nd yet from all the enemy there was not heard a sound.
he lovers sang their last duet, in danger of their lives—
or the foe was armed with toasting forks and cruel carving knives.

hen GILBERT gave the signal to his fierce Mongolian horde;
Vith a frightful burst of fireworks the Chinks they swarmed aboard.
bandoning their sampans, and their pullaways and junks,
hey battened down the hatches on the crew within their bunks.

Then Griddlebone she gave a screech, for she was badly skeered;
I am sorry to admit it, but she quickly disappeared.
She probably escaped with ease, I'm sure she was not drowned—
But a serried ring of flashing steel Growltiger did surround.

The ruthless foe pressed forward, in stubborn rank on rank;
Growltiger to his vast surprise was forced to walk the plank.
He who a hundred victims had driven to that drop,
At the end of all his crimes was forced to go ker-flip, ker-flop.

Oh there was joy in Wapping when the news flew through the land;
At Maidenhead and Henley there was dancing on the strand.
Rats were roasted whole at Brentford, and at Victoria Dock,
And a day of celebration was commanded in Bangkok.

CAT!

Eleanor Farjeon

Cat!
Scat!
Atter her, atter her,
Sleeky flatterer,
Spitfire chatterer,
Scatter her, scatter her
    Off her mat!
    Wuff!
    Wuff!
    Treat her rough!

Git her, git her,
Whiskery spitter!
Catch her, catch her,
Green-eyed scratcher!
    Slathery
    Slithery
    Hisser,
    Don't miss her!
Run till you're dithery,
    Hithery
    Thithery
    Pfitts! pfitts!
    How she spits!
    Spitch! Spatch!
    Can't she scratch!
Scritching the bark
Of the sycamore-tree,
She's reached her ark
And's hissing at me
    Pfitts! pfitts!
    Wuff! wuff!
    Scat,
    Cat!
    That's
    That!

THE SINGING CAT

Stevie Smith

It was a little captive cat
    Upon a crowded train
His mistress takes him from his box
    To ease his fret and pain.

She holds him tight upon her knee
    The graceful animal
And all the people look at him
    He is so beautiful.

But oh he pricks and oh he prods
    And turns upon her knee
Then lifteth up his innocent voice
    In plaintive melody.

He lifteth up his innocent voice
    He lifteth up, he singeth
And to each human countenance
    A smile of grace he bringeth.

He lifteth up his innocent paw
    Upon her breast he clingeth
And everybody cries, Behold
    The cat, the cat that singeth.

He lifteth up his innocent voice
    He lifteth up, he singeth
And all the people warm themselves
    In the love his beauty bringeth.

OLD SHELLOVER

Walter De la Mare

'Come!' said Old Shellover.
'What?' says Creep.
'The horny old Gardener's fast asleep;
The fat cock Thrush
To his nest has gone;

And the dew shines bright
In the rising Moon;
Old Sallie Worm from her hole doth peep:
'Come!' said Old Shellover.
'Ay!' said Creep.

HARVEST MOUSE

Clive Sansom

A sleek, brown acrobat, he climbs
The golden cornstalk till it sways
And sags beneath him. As it swings,
His tail-end twines a neighbour stalk
And balancing with tail and claw
He climbs aloft until he finds
The crisp, ripe, bristly ear of corn;
Then lies along its tilting length,
As if all corn-ears were created
For mice to nibble at . . . and nibbles.

THE CAT

W. H. Davies

Within that porch, across the way,
I see two naked eyes this night;
Two eyes that neither shut nor blink,
Searching my face with a green light.

But cats to me are strange, so strange—
I cannot sleep if one is near;
And though I'm sure I see those eyes
I'm not so sure a body's there!

RAGS

John Walsh

Rags is a good dog,
The best I've had;
Yet there are words — a special few —
Which drive him mad.

They drive him mad
By their very sound:
Words like 'ball' and 'park' and 'lead'
And 'football ground'.

He whines at the door
To be set free;
He snatches the ball: he dribbles in dog-
   like ecstasy

Then off like an arrow
Straight to its mark—
Off and away to the broad spaces
Of the green park!

Splashing through puddles;
Scattering the earth;
Turning to greet me: rocketing skyward
For all he's worth!

Believe me or not,
It's pretty poor fun
When Rags has made up his mind to take
Me for a run!

Never behind me—
Always before!
Till I cry for mercy, and make a dash
For the café door;

For the café door—
Where I leave him tied,
Fighting the board which says 'No Dogs
Allowed Inside';

Leaping for joy
When I come out;
Then on again to the football-field
With bark and shout;

Till we squat at last
By the muddy stream,
And slowly, and piece by tiny piece,
He shares my ice-cream!

DOWN THE STREAM
THE SWANS ALL GLIDE

Spike Milligan

Down the stream the swans all glide;
It's quite the cheapest way to ride.
Their legs get wet,
Their tummies wetter:
I think after all
The bus is better.

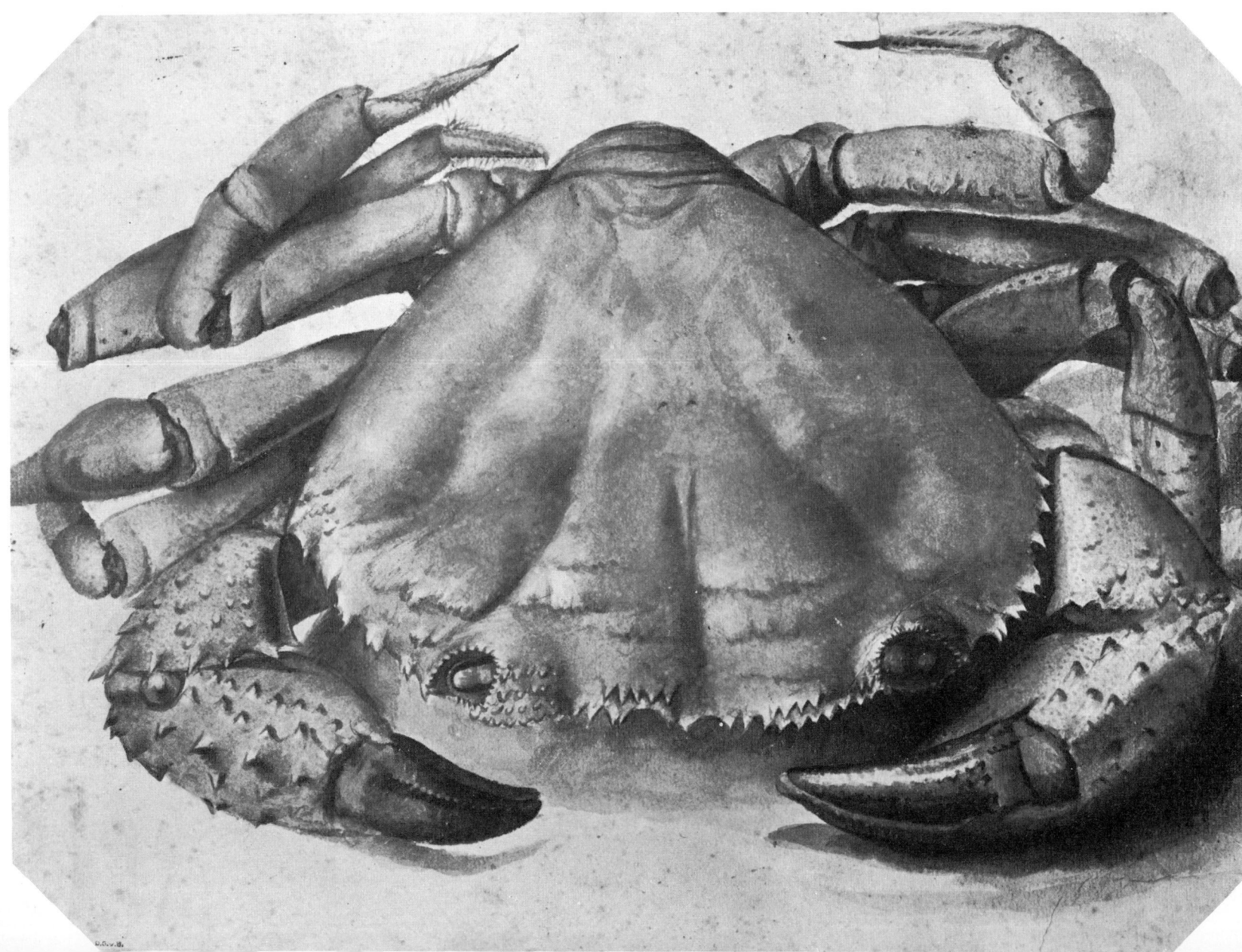

THE GIANT CRAB

John Walsh

Along the steep wall at the old pier's side,
The scavenging crabs come up with the tide.
'Want to catch one? It's easy! You don't need a thing
But a stone, and some fish, and some odd bits of string;
Look here now — I'll show you. First fetch that big stone—
The one with the hole through — the cobble- shaped one;
Now join up your string — all the odd bits you've got—
Loop one end through the stone, and tie tight in a knot;
Then cram in these bits of stale fish for a bait . . .
Ready? Over she goes!
     Now you've only to wait!'

Not long!

There's a tiny commotion below in the water;
There's a shout from above as the line becomes tauter;
There's a hauling up, hand over hand, until — whee-ee-ee!—
A monster-great crab swings clear of the sea—
All legs and sharp claws, hanging desperately on,
His pincers stuck fast through the hole in the stone!
'Quick, get him!' 'No hurry! He's stupid — he'll cling
Till we land him. Pull steady, and don't break the string . . .
Whoops! Over he comes! Give the string a sharp shake,
And he'll let go his hold and fall down on his back.'

Well done!

'Now who'll pick him up?' 'Not me!' 'No, not me!
It's you said you fancied a crab for your tea!'
'*I* said? I don't want him!' 'Hey, Billy, he's yours!
Come along and make friends with him!'
'What? With those claws?
I'm not touching him yet; I'll wait till he's dead!'
'You boil them alive; that's what my mother said;
They scream in the saucepan.' 'This one would get out:
He'd flop to the floor and go scrambling about—
He'd crawl on the baby; he'd frighten the cat;
Why, he could do anything with claws like that!
He could jab you—'
     'Hey, somebody! Lend me that stick:
Hook him by the legs and pitch him back quick!'

Whe-e-e-ew! Sploosh! He's gone! . . .

Thank goodness!

EGG O EGG

Keith Bosley

Egg O egg
shape of mouth
saying O

not speaking
keeping your
secrets
    O
little world
keeping life
warm and dumb

until *crack!*
and the world
begins
    beak
pecks and wet
from within
squeaks
    a chick

COWS

James Reeves

Half the time they munched the grass, and all the time
  they lay
Down in the water-meadows, the lazy month of May,
    A-chewing,
    A-mooing,
  To pass the hours away.

  'Nice weather,' said the brown cow.
    'Ah,' said the white.
  'Grass is very tasty.'
    'Grass is all right.'

Half the time they munched the grass, and all the time
  they lay
Down in the water-meadows, the lazy month of May,
    A-chewing,
    A-mooing,
  To pass the hours away.

  'Rain coming,' said the brown cow.
    'Ah,' said the white.
  'Flies is very tiresome.'
    'Flies bite.'

Half the time they munched the grass, and all the time
  they lay
Down in the water-meadows, the lazy month of May,
    A-chewing,
    A-mooing,
  To pass the hours away.

  'Time to go,' said the brown cow.
    'Ah,' said the white.
  'Nice chat.' 'Very pleasant.'
    'Night.' 'Night.'

Half the time they munched the grass, and all the time
  they lay
Down in the water-meadows, the lazy month of May,
    A-chewing,
    A-mooing,
  To pass the hours away.

THE DUCK AND THE KANGAROO

Edward Lear

I

Said the Duck to the Kangaroo,
  'Good gracious! how you hop!
Over the fields and the water too,
  As if you never would stop!
My life is a bore in this nasty pond,
And I long to go out in the world beyond!
  I wish I could hop like you!'
  Said the Duck to the Kangaroo.

II

'Please give me a ride on your back!'
  Said the Duck to the Kangaroo.
'I would sit quite still, and say nothing but "Quack,"
  The whole of the long day through!
And we'd go to the Dee, and the Jelly Bo Lee,
Over the land, and over the sea;—
  Please take me a ride! O do!'
  Said the Duck to the Kangaroo.

III

Said the Kangaroo to the Duck,
  'This requires some little reflection;
Perhaps on the whole it might bring me luck,
  And there seems but one objection,
Which is, if you'll let me speak so bold,
Your feet are unpleasantly wet and cold,
And would probably give me the roo-
  Matiz!' said the Kangaroo.

IV

Said the Duck, 'As I sate on the rocks,
  I have thought over that completely,
And I bought four pairs of worsted socks
  Which fit my web-feet neatly.
And to keep out the cold I've bought a cloak,
And every day a cigar I'll smoke,
  All to follow my own dear true
  Love of a Kangaroo!'

V

Said the Kangaroo, 'I'm ready!
  All in the moonlight pale;
But to balance me well, dear Duck, sit steady!
  And quite at the end of my tail!'
So away they went with a hop and a bound,
And they hopped the whole world three times round
  And who so happy,—O who,
  As the Duck and the Kangaroo?

HURT NO LIVING THING

Christina Rossetti

Hurt no living thing;
Ladybird, nor butterfly,
Nor moth with dusty wing,
Nor cricket chirping cheerily,
Nor grasshopper so light of leap,
Nor dancing gnat, nor beetle fat,
Nor harmless worms that creep.

Talking and Writing

—Do you have a pet animal? What pets are the most popular in your class? In the poem about *Rags*, page 86. the little boy shows how much he likes being taken for a walk by his dog. What do you like *best* about pets? What are the *worst* things about having a pet? Write about a pet animal and about the good, bad and funny things it does.

— Do you have any creatures in school — gerbils, rabbits, stick insects? If you do, look very closely at the creature you like best and try to describe it by writing about one thing at a time and saying what it is like. So, for example, you could start by writing

   "The rabbit's fur is like . . . .

   His eyes are like . . . ."

and so on until you have completed your poem.

— The picture on page 93 shows a baby foal. Have you ever seen a baby animal? Can you write about it? If you like horses and want to write about the foal, look carefully at the picture as you write.

— Edward Lear's poem about *The Duck and the Kangaroo* on page 92 is fun to read aloud especially if three people share the reading, with one voice telling the story and the other two reading the animals. Perhaps you could try it and some of you could, in pairs, pretend to be the animals and mime their journey.

— If you read the poem on page 84 aloud, you can hear the sounds of the frightened cat chased by the dog.

Can you find words with the right sounds to describe a dog-fight? Perhaps you could suggest words to be put on the blackboard and arrange them so that they make a poem called 'Dogfight'.

Author Index

Printed in Great Britain for
Hodder and Stoughton Educational,
a division of Hodder and Stoughton Ltd,
Mill Road, Dunton Green, Sevenoaks, Kent,
by Hazell Watson & Viney Ltd. Aylesbury, Bucks

Acknowledgements

Thanks are due to the following authors (or their agents or trustees) and publishers for permission to reprint poems: pages 54 and 90, Keith Bosley, 'Cat' and 'Egg O Egg' from *And I Dance* (Angus and Robertson, Sydney); page 40, Lewis Carroll, © Trustees of the Dodgson Estate from *The Wasp in the Wig*, (Macmillan, London and Basingstoke); pages 46, 65, 78 and 74, Charles Causley, 'Colonel Fazackerley', 'Old Mrs Thing-um-e-bob', 'Figgie Hobbin' and 'Green Man in the Garden' from *Collected Poems* and *Figgie Hobbin* (Macmillan, London and Basingstoke); page 50, Kevin Crossley—Holland, 'Riddle' (Novello and Company Ltd); page 58, Roald Dahl, 'Television' from *Charlie and the Chocolate Factory* (George Allen and Unwin Ltd); page 85, W H Davies, © Mrs H M Davies, 'The Cat' from *The Complete Poems of W H Davies* (Jonathan Cape Ltd); pages 53, 52, 62, 85 and 68, Walter De la Mare, © The Society of Authors for the Literary Trustees of Walter De la Mare, 'The Snowflake', 'Seeds', 'Hide and Seek', 'Miss T', 'The Old Sailor', 'Old Shellover' and 'Off the Ground' from *Secret Laughter* and *Selected Poems*; page 82, T S Eliot, 'Growltiger's Last Stand' from *Old Possum's Book of Practical Cats* (Faber and Faber Ltd); page 29, Eleanor Farjeon, 'Peter' from *The Children's Bells* (Oxford University Press); pages 52 and 84, Eleanor Farjeon, 'The Tide in the River' and 'Cat' from *Silver Sand and Snow* (Michael Joseph Ltd); pages 64 and 76, Michael Flanders and Donald Swann, 'A Transport of Delight (The Omnibus)' and 'The Spider' from *The Songs of Michael Flanders and Donald Swann* (Elm Tree Books); pages 14, 22, 24, 34 and 35, Roy Fuller, © 1977, 'End of Girl's First Tooth', 'A Boy's Friend', 'Horrible Things', 'The National Union of Children' and 'The National Association of Parents' from *Poor Roy* and *Seen Grandpa Lately?* (André Deutsch Ltd); page 33, Ted Hughes, 'My Aunt' from *Meet My Folks* (Faber and Faber Ltd); pages 23, 24 and 62, Elizabeth Jennings, 'Friends', 'The Secret Brother', and 'Old People' from *The Secret Brother* (Macmillan, London and Basingstoke); page 60, Rudyard Kipling, © The National Trust, 'The Camel's Hump' from *The Just So Stories* (Macmillan, London and Basingstoke); pages 10 and 13, James Kirkup, 'The Broken Toys' and 'Who's That'; pages 8, 20, 21 and 31, Brian Lee, © 1976, 'Pockets', 'Cold Feet', 'Words' and 'My Back-Scratcher' from *Late Home* (Kestrel Books); page 2, Roger McGough, 'Watchwords' from *Watchwords* (Jonathan Cape Ltd); page 32, Roger McGough © 1974, 'Uncle Fergie' from *Sporting Relations* (Eyre Methuen); page 87, Spike Milligan, 'Down the Stream the Swans All Glide' from *Silly Verse for Kids* (Dennis Dobson); page 44, Ogden Nash, © The Estate of the Late Ogden Nash, 'The Wendigo'; pages 72 and 73, Brian Patten, © 1977, 'The Lion's Worst Enemy' and 'The Crane and The Bone of Contention' from *The Sly Cormorant and the Fishes* (Kestrel Books); page 11, Sylvia Plath, © Ted Hughes 1976, 'The Right Kind of Bed' from *The Bed Book* (Faber and Faber Ltd); page 40, James Reeves, 'The Doze' from *Prefabulous Animiles* (William Heinemann Ltd); page 91, James Reeves, © 1952, 'Cows' from *The Blackbird in the Lilac* (Oxford University Press); page 45, Alan Riddell, 'Child's Game' from *Eclipse* (Calder and Boyars Ltd);

pages 28, 29, 12, 55 and 22, Michael Rosen © 1975 and 1977, 'If You Don't Put Your Shoes On', 'Father Says', 'I'm Alone in the Evening', 'My Dad's Thumb' and 'I went Out and Looked About' from *Mind Your Own Business* and *Wouldn't You Like to Know* (André Deutsch Ltd); pages 63 and 55, Clive Sansom, 'The Dustman' and 'Intruder' from *Golden Unicorn* (Metheun); page 85, Clive Sansom, 'Harvest House' from *An English Year* (Chatto and Windus); page 84, Stevie Smith, 'The Singing Cat' from *The Collected Poems of Stevie Smith* (James MacGibbon and Allen Lane); page 51, J R R Tolkien, 'Riddle' from *The Hobbit* (George Allen and Unwin Ltd); pages 14, 10, 17, 80 and 89, John Walsh, © Mrs A M Walsh, 'Joan Who Hates Parties', 'Bus to School', 'Lost in a Shop', 'Rags', and 'The Giant Crab'; page 79, recipe for 'Figgie Hobbin' from *British Cookery* edited by Lizzie Boyd (Croom Helm Ltd);

The authors and publishers wish to thank the following for permission to reproduce illustrations: Back cover, and pages 8, 9, 6, 25, 29, 33, 34, 35, 55, 90, Alan Hayward, Senior Lecturer in Communications and Learning Resources, King Alfred's College, Winchester, photographs taken for *Watchwords 1*. Pages 1, and 71, Robert Mackay, photographs taken for *Watchwords 1*. Page 60, Miriam Austerman, from *Austerman's Animals* (John Hillelson Agency Ltd); page 10, Ian Berry, 'Whitechapel' (John Hillelson Agency Ltd); page 82, Janine Billois, 'Cat' (John Hillelson Agency Ltd); page 54, Serge Bois-Prevost (John Hillelson Agency Ltd); page 41, from Lewis Carroll's *The Wasp in the Wig* (Trustees of the Dodgson Estate and Macmillan, London and Basingstoke); page 88, Albrecht Durer, 'Crab' (Museum Boymans — van Beuningen, Rotterdam); page 86, Elliott Erwitt, 'Son of Bitch' (John Hillelson Agency Ltd); pages 51 and 52, M C Escher (Haags Gemeentemuseum); pages 76 and 77, from *The Songs of Michael Flanders and Donald Swann*, 'The Spider' (St George's Press); page 32, Terry Gilliam, 'Uncle Fergie' from *Sporting Relations* (Eyre Methuen); page 93, Bert Hardy, 'Birth of a Foal' (John Hillelson Agency Ltd); pages 14 and 23, Michael Hardy (John Hillelson Agency Ltd); page 12, Abigail Heyman, 'Playing in the Attic' from *Growing Up Female* (John Hillelson Agency Ltd); page 65, L S Lowry, © Mrs Carol Spiers, 'Lady with a Handbag'; page 72, (The Mansell Collection); page 63, J Roan, 'Harvey Street and Inhabitants' (Northampton Mercury); page 74, the Revd. Canon E Eric Roberts, 'Jack in Green' in Southwell Minster; page 45, Paolo Robino, 'Volkswagen with Hands and Feet'; page 20, Carl Uytterhaegen, 'Children on and around Fallen Tree'; page 80, J Whitworth, 'Owl with Rat'; page 59, Gluyas Williams, 'Portrait of a Small Boy Reading' from *The Best of Gluyas Williams* (Dover Publications).

The publishers have made every effort to trace copyright-holders, but if they have inadvertently overlooked any they will be pleased to make the necessary arrangements at the first opportunity.

Answers to 'Riddles' on page 51:
Teeth   Wind   Fish